FOLK DANCES OF EUROPEAN COUNTRIES

The Folk Dance Library

ANNE SCHLEY DUGGAN

JEANETTE SCHLOTTMANN

ABBIE RUTLEDGE

☆

The Teaching of Folk Dance

Folk Dances of Scandinavia

Folk Dances of European Countries

Folk Dances of the British Isles

Folk Dances of the United States and Mexico

☆

German

Swiss

Swiss

Swiss and German

Bavarian

The Folk Dance Library
Folk Dances
OF EUROPEAN COUNTRIES

ANNE SCHLEY DUGGAN

JEANETTE SCHLOTTMANN

ABBIE RUTLEDGE

THE RONALD PRESS COMPANY · NEW YORK

5

Dedication

To Stella Owsley, our mutual friend and a genuine lover of the folk arts, who has contributed richly through her aid and encouragement to the preparation of *The Folk Dance Library*—and to our students of folk dance everywhere.

The Authors

Preface

The Folk Dance Library was undertaken by the authors as the result of innumerable requests directed both to them and to the publishers from teachers at all educational levels and from recreation leaders for a presentation of folk dance materials immediately adaptable to the teaching of folk dance as a cultural subject as well as a form of motor activity. It is designed, therefore, to provide teachers of folk dance in schools and colleges, recreationalists, leaders of folk dance in churches and civic organizations, and all individuals everywhere who are interested in this fascinating heritage of our civilization with a more intimate acquaintance with folk dance materials as a means of enriching their study. The underlying purposes of the authors in undertaking the development of *The Folk Dance Library* are:

First, to present a collection of folk dances representative of as many nations as possible with clear directions and musical accompaniments for each of the dances analyzed.

Second, to arrange the folk dances presented in units of organization according to specific geographical regions with representative dances of varying degrees of difficulty within each unit. *The Folk Dance Library* includes the directions and music for eighty-three folk dances grouped into seven regional units for their presentation along with the analyses of fundamental and basic steps, formations, and directions employed in the descriptions of the dances themselves. This organization of materials into units serves the two-fold purpose of providing enough folk dance material to insure more than a sporadic and superficial acquaintance with the characteristic folk dances of the countries represented and of providing enough folk dance material within each unit to serve as a nucleus for folk dance parties, festivals, and other culminating projects. In each unit, therefore, there are some very simple dances for general participation as well as others which will prove challenging for demonstration purposes for those of more advanced skill. The dances listed in each unit are arranged in order of difficulty and include dances for boys and men only, for girls and women only, and for mixed groups comprised of both sexes. The material incorporates dances which are ceremonial and ritualistic in origin as well as those which are highly social and recreational in nature.

Third, to present background materials in conjunction with each unit of dances so that folk dance may be correlated with and integrated more effectively into the curriculum as a whole to the end that, through folk dance, students may gain a better understanding of their neighbors in the world at large. Each unit includes, therefore, (1) a brief résumé of the history and characteristics of the peoples whose dances are analyzed; (2) a survey of general topographical and climatic conditions of the given region and a map with the placement of towns, villages, rivers, and mountains directly associated with the origins of the dances which follow; and (3) an overview of the folk dances of the specific country or countries described, significant holidays or festivals commemorated, forms of musical accompaniments, and traditional costumes with a colored costume plate illustrating authentic and typical costumes worn by dancers of the particular region in question. Wherever possible, the origins of the individual dances comprising each unit are pointed out with respect to the significance of their titles, formations, and basic steps. This background material is necessarily brief but suggestive of a wealth of information which, properly utilized, is significant because it is reflected in the dances themselves and should insure, therefore, the teaching of folk dance as a folk art. The bibliographies included in each of the volumes provide sources for further study.

Fourth, to foster a vitalized feeling of nationalism in every country and to demonstrate through folklore the close cultural ties shared by the peoples of all nations, thereby promoting a broader concept of internationalism.

Fifth, to indoctrinate boys and girls and men and women everywhere with the idea that participation in the folk dances of all countries is an indispensable phase of their education, affording not only invaluable training in rhythm and basic motor skills but also the means of realizing all sorts of concomitant or associated learnings as well—folklore, legends, customs, costumes, traditions, holidays and feast days, folk songs, folk music and other related arts—to the end that folk dance may serve as an enriching, leisure-time activity for those of all ages.

The Folk Dance Library consists of five volumes variously entitled *The Teaching of Folk Dance, Folk Dances of Scandinavia, Folk Dances of European Countries, Folk Dances of the British Isles,* and *Folk Dances of the United States and Mexico.* In preparing the manuscript for *The Teaching of Folk Dance,* the purpose of the authors was to summarize and to apply to the field of folk dance—rather than to duplicate in any sort of technical detail—available materials in educational methodology including those in the special field of testing. Fundamental principles for the production of folk festivals and folk dance parties as culminating projects in conjunction with the folk dance program in schools, colleges, and recreation centers are listed with suggestive outlines for the production of two illustrative folk festivals and a typical folk dance party. This particular book in the series of five volumes was planned, therefore, as an overview to folk dance leadership to be used in conjunction with each of the remaining four volumes comprising *The Folk Dance Library.*

This collection of folk dances is the result of many years of study and firsthand experience with ethnological groups in Mexico and in all parts of this country. It includes, therefore, some folk dances that are old favorites appearing in other collections and a number of dances which have not been published previously. The authors have endeavored throughout to present authentic versions of the folk dances analyzed and to describe them in such a way that they will be interpreted and danced in the manner of the ethnic groups from whom they were learned. Wherever versions presented differ from those appearing in other collections, the reader is reminded that folk dance, like language, often gives rise to variations in the same manner in which dialects vary in different sections of a given country.

The authors wish to express their gratitude to the many individuals who have contributed through their aid and encouragement to the development of *The Folk Dance Library.* Specifically, they are deeply indebted to Mary Campbell, Texas State College for Women, and to Esther Allen Bremer, Teachers College, Columbia University, for their accurate recording of the various folk melodies accompanying the dances and for their arrangements of these melodies into the piano accompaniments for the dances analyzed; to the two gifted artists at the Texas State College for Women who contributed the illustrations which add immeasurably to the purpose of *The Folk Dance Library* as a whole—Lura B. Kendrick for the colored pictorial maps and for the colored costume plates for each unit and Coreen Spellman for the brush drawings, black and white maps, and illustrative diagrams; to the historians on the faculty of the Texas State College for Women who read the sections devoted to geographical, historical, and sociological background material for the various units, to June Anderson and Claire Mae Jenkins, major students in the Department of Health, Physical Education, and Recreation of the Texas State College for Women for their service as patient and skillful models for the illustrators; and to Bette Jean Reed for her invaluable assistance in the preparation of the manuscript. The authors are grateful to the publishers who have granted permission for the use of direct quotations.

It is the sincere hope of the authors that *The Folk Dance Library* will prove a source of aid to those whose needs were anticipated in its purposes, and that folk dance will become a living and enriching folk art to boys and girls as well as to men and women everywhere.

ANNE SCHLEY DUGGAN
JEANETTE SCHLOTTMANN
ABBIE RUTLEDGE
Texas State College for Women, Denton, Texas

Table of Contents

Folk Dances of European Countries

Introduction

The specific units into which this collection of folk dances is divided are preceded by the following introductory materials to serve as aids in the use of the volume. These materials comprise three sections:

1. *Explanation of Terms, Counting, Music and Diagrams*—which defines the specific meaning with which the authors have used certain words and phrases in the analysis of dances throughout the volume and explains the system of counting steps and the coordination of the music and diagrams with the analyses of the dances included.

2. *Analysis of Basic Steps, Figures, Positions and Formations*—which clarifies the manner in which steps, figures, positions, and formations commonly used in folk dance are to be executed as they occur in the analyses of dances included in this volume.

3. *Pronunciation of Foreign Words*—which is presented in an effort to encourage teachers of folk dance to give background materials to students along with dances from each of the units included without the stumbling hesitancy which frequently accompanies the pronunciation of foreign words as they necessarily appear in such discussions.

Each of these three sections is preceded by its own directions for proper interpretation. The authors caution those using this volume to adhere to the analysis of steps and positions in order to achieve an accurate performance of any specific dance.

A map of general topographical interest including the placement of towns, villages, rivers, and mountains directly associated with the origins of the specific folk dances which follow precedes each geographical unit in *The Folk Dance Library*. Each unit is accompanied also by a colored costume plate, illustrating authentic and typical costumes worn by the dancers of the particular region in question. These supplementary materials have been included to further the integration of folk dance in the school or college curriculum or in the recreational program. A classified bibliography may be found at the end of this volume which includes the titles of books and articles which served as source materials for the authors and which may be utilized to advantage by those who wish to explore further information pertinent to each unit.

The authors believe that careful study of these aids to insure accurate interpretation of the folk dance materials which follow will reward those who do so with greater facility and satisfaction in learning and teaching from the various volumes of *The Folk Dance Library*.

EXPLANATION OF TERMS, COUNTING, MUSIC AND DIAGRAMS

Clockwise: a direction of progression in a circular formation or for turning in place in which dancers move in the same direction as the hands of a clock.

Counterclockwise: a direction of progression in a circular formation or for turning in place in which dancers move in a direction opposite to the hands of a clock.

L and R: abbreviations used for "left" and "right," respectively, to designate feet on which steps are taken, arms with or directions in which movements are made. To turn L or R is to turn in the direction of the L or R shoulder as indicated in the analysis of the specific dance.

Front, Back, R and L walls: directions so called with reference to dancers' positions facing the front of the room or gymnasium. The walls at their back and on their right and left are thereafter designated as Back, R, and L, walls, respectively, regardless of their changed positions in the course of a dance.

Counting steps: In the main, the dances analyzed in this volume fall into the more common meters of 2/4, 3/4, 4/4, and 6/8. In interpreting the meter signatures, attention is called to the fact that the numerator designates the number of counts to be given to one measure of music and the denominator indicates the kind of note to receive one beat or count. So that the rhythm of the steps may be fitted accurately to the music, each part of the analysis of the steps is given a definite time value. For example, if four even movements occur in each measure of music in 4/4 time, each movement should be counted 1, 2, 3, 4. If eight movements of equal time value occur in a similar measure, they should be counted 1&, 2&, 3&, 4&. Movements of shorter duration than may be taken care of with the & count should be counted ah. These counts—1, &, and ah—correspond respectively to the time values of quarter, eighth, and sixteenth notes in music. Further attention is called to the fact that although most of the dances are danced to one meter only, in some the various parts of the dance have different meters for each part. In a few dances, a single measure of a different meter is interpolated. In the case of the English dances with very ancient meters, the signatures are more unusual, i.e., 2/2, 12/16, 9/8, *et cetera*. These are counted in the same way, however, as explained above.

Use of Music: The measures of the music for each dance have been keyed to the analyses of the dances so that the music for each part of a specific dance is indicated in the column entitled "measures." The pianist and teacher will experience no difficulty in fitting the dances to the music if they will match measures as well as counts with the analysis of each dance.

Attention is also called to the metronome marks at the beginning of the music for each dance and to the fact that, in some dances, the metronome mark changes for various parts within a single dance, indicating a change of tempo for these parts. These specifications as to tempo should be carefully observed for maximum joy in participation and appreciation of the dances. The metronome marks represent in each instance the optimum tempo for performing each dance. When steps are difficult, it is possible that the established tempo may not be used until the dancers gain adequate proficiency in performance.

Diagrams: In the diagrams throughout the book, circles are used to indicate positions of women and squares for positions of men. Unless otherwise indicated, a straight line denotes the path of progression for a man and a broken line the path for a woman.

ANALYSIS OF BASIC STEPS, FIGURES, POSITIONS AND FORMATIONS
USED IN THE DESCRIPTION OF THE DANCES

For purposes of uniformity, the basic steps included in this section are analyzed beginning R and moving forward. However, they should be performed according to the foot designated in each specific dance included in this collection, and in a forward, backward, sideward, or turning direction as indicated.

Basic steps are analyzed for each of the meters in which they are danced in the various folk dances themselves.

BASIC STEPS AND FIGURES

Change step: an uneven step in duple meter which may be analyzed as follows:

	COUNTS		MEASURES
	2/4	4/4	
Step forward R	1	1	
Close L beside R, taking weight L	&	2	
Step forward R	2	3	
Rise to ball of R foot, swinging L leg forward. Sometimes the rise to the ball of the R foot is carried into a hop	&	4	1

To repeat *change step,* begin L.

Close: a movement in which the free foot is brought to the foot supporting the body weight which may or may not be transferred to the free foot, according to specific directions in the dance analyzed.

Curtsey: a form of address for women usually made by touching the toe of the L foot behind the heel of the R foot and bending both knees, at the same time bowing the head.

Cut: a movement made by springing onto the free foot to replace the foot with the weight, at the same time swinging the latter forward, backward or to the side, as designated, with a sharp cutting motion.

Flat: a step made onto the entire foot with less accent than a stamp.

Grand R and L: a weaving figure which is performed in a circular formation. Partners face, men facing counterclockwise and women clockwise, and pass each other by right shoulders to face a new person whom they pass by left shoulders. For a complete Grand R and L, all continue passing alternately by right and left sides (men continuing to progress counterclockwise, women clockwise) until original positions are regained, each person having passed own partner a second time. Hands may or may not be clasped in passing as indicated in the specific dance. The number of persons passed depends upon the analysis of the dance.

Hop: with weight on R, spring into the air and land R.

Hopsa step: an uneven step in duple meter which may be analyzed as follows:

	COUNTS 2/4	MEASURES
Spring sideward onto R foot	1	
Touch L toe in front of R foot, taking weight L lightly	&	
Step R in place	2	
Hold	&	1

To repeat *hopsa step*, begin L.

Jump: with weight on both feet, spring into the air and land again on both feet.

Leap: with weight L, push off floor with that foot and into the air, swinging R forward to receive weight in landing.

Mazurka step: an even step in triple meter which may be analyzed as follows:

	COUNTS 3/4	MEASURES
Stamp or step forward R	1	
Step L beside R, swinging R leg forward	2	
Hop L, bending R knee, R foot lifted off floor	3	1

To repeat the *mazurka step*, begin R.

Pivot-turn step: a turning step involving a step and pivot on alternate feet with a half-turn on each pivot, thus requiring two pivot steps for one complete turn. When danced by couples in shoulder-waist position, partners lean away from each other from the waist, keeping arms straight, and dance with feet in a wide stride, knees relatively straight, and close to partner's feet. This step may be danced in either duple or triple meter, according to the directions of the specific dance in which it occurs.

Polka step: an uneven step in duple meter which may be analyzed as follows:

	COUNTS 2/4	6/8	MEASURES
Hop R	ah	6	
Step forward L	1	1	
Close R to L, taking weight R	&	3	
Step forward L	2	4	1

To repeat the *polka step*, begin with a hop L.

R and L Chain: See *Grand R and L.*

R and L hand mills:

  Mill: a design, usually formed by two couples, in which each of the four dancers joins R hands with the dancer diagonally across the set to form a R hand mill and all move around clockwise or joins L hands to form a L hand mill so that all move around counterclockwise.

Running step: an even step for progression in any direction by stepping on alternate feet and pushing off the floor with more elevation than in walking.

Schottische step: an even step in duple meter which may be analyzed as follows:

	COUNTS		MEASURES	
	2/4	4/4	2/4	4/4
Regular				
Step forward R	1	1		
Close L to R, taking weight L	2	2	1	
Step forward R	1	3		
Hop R, swinging L foot forward	2	4	2	1
Running				
3 running steps forward, R, L, R	1,2,1	1,2,3		
Hop R, swinging L foot forward	2	4	2	1

To repeat *schottische step*, begin L.
NOTE: *Schottische steps* are danced in a brisk, vigorous manner with a firm, erect position of the body and with a light quality of elevation.

Scuff: weight L, swing the R leg forward, R knee bent, striking the R heel against the floor and into the air.

Set: a term used to designate a specified number of dancers comprising a given formation.

Skip step: an uneven step in duple meter which may be analyzed as follows:

	COUNTS			MEASURES
	2/4	4/4	6/8	
Step R	1	1	1	
Hop R	ah	ah	3	
Repeat, beginning L	2 ah	2 ah, 3 ah, 4 ah, etc.	4,6	1

To continue *skip step*, begin alternately R, L, etc.

Slide: an uneven step in duple meter for progression sideward in which the body is in the air most of the time and in which the feet are not always in contact with the floor:

	COUNTS			MEASURES
	2/4	4/4	6/8	
Step sideward R	1	1	1	
Close L to R, taking weight L	ah	ah	3	
Repeat	2 ah	2 ah, 3 ah, 4 ah, etc.	4,6	1

To continue *slide step*, begin R.

Spring: a transfer of weight from one foot to another by pushing off floor and into air with foot supporting body weight and landing on free foot. Step may be taken forward, sideward, or backward and involves less elevation than a leap but more than a running step.

Stamp: a forceful step made onto the entire foot which may or may not involve a transfer of weight as indicated in the specific dances in which the *stamp* occurs.

Step-hop: an even step in duple meter which may be analyzed as follows:

	COUNTS			MEASURES
	2/4	4/4	6/8	
	1	1	1	
Step forward R	&	2	4	
Hop R	2&	3,4	1,4	1
Repeat, beginning L				

To continue *step-hop*, begin alternately R, L, etc.

Treading step: small steps danced high on the balls of the feet in rapid succession.

Two-step: an uneven step in duple meter which may be analyzed as follows:

	COUNTS		MEASURES
	2/4	4/4	
	1	1	
Step forward R	&	2	
Close L to R, taking weight L	2	3	
Step forward R	&	4	1
Hold			

To repeat *two-step*, begin L.

Varsovienne step: an even step in triple meter which may be analyzed as follows:

	COUNTS	MEASURES
	3/4	
3 steps, R, L, R	1,2,3	1
Place L heel to floor, without weight	1	
Hold	2,3	1

To repeat *varsovienne step*, begin L.

Walking step: an even step for progression in any direction in which steps are taken on alternate feet, the supporting foot remaining in contact with the floor until the transfer of weight is completed.

Waltz step: an even step in triple meter which may be analyzed as follows:

	COUNTS	MEASURES
	3/4	
Step forward R	1	
Step forward L	2	
Close R to L, taking weight R	3	1

To repeat *waltz step*, begin L.

Waltz balance step: an even step in triple meter which may be analyzed as follows:

	COUNTS 3/4	MEASURES
Step forward R, bending R knee	1	
Step L beside R, rising on ball of L foot	2	
Step R in place beside L	3	1

To repeat *waltz balance step*, begin L.

BASIC POSITIONS AND FORMATIONS

Closed social dance positions as illustrated in Plate 1, page 20.

Open social dance position, outside hands on hips as illustrated in Plate 2, page 21.

Open social dance position, outside hands joined and extended forward as illustrated in Plate 3, page 22.

Partners side by side, inside hands joined at shoulder level as illustrated in Plate 4, page 23.

Shoulder-waist position: Partners face each other squarely, face-to-face. The woman places both hands on her partner's shoulders with very straight arms while he takes hold of her waist by placing both hands on either side with straight arms. Keeping face-to-face throughout, the two dancers lean strongly away from each other in order to supply the centrifugal force necessary to achieve the turns indicated in the step-hop, change-step, two-step, and the waltz and polka steps analyzed for this position in various folk dances. (See Finnish couple on Scandinavian Costume Plate in the volume of *The Folk Dance Library* entitled *Folk Dances of Scandinavia.*)

Stride position: a standing position in which the feet are apart. In a forward stride, one foot is in advance of the other. In a side stride, the feet are out to the side.

Double circle, facing clockwise as illustrated in Diagram 1, page 24.

Double circle, facing counterclockwise as illustrated in Diagram 2, page 24.

Double circle, partners facing as illustrated in Diagram 3, page 25.

Duple minor set: Term used to indicate sets of four dancers within a larger longways or circular formation.

Longways set, facing up as illustrated in Diagram 4, page 25.

Longways set, partners facing as illustrated in Diagram 5, page 26.

Single circle, facing in as illustrated in Diagram 6, page 26.

Single circle, partners facing as illustrated in Diagram 7, page 27.

Quadrille or Square Formation as illustrated in Diagram 8, page 27.

Plate 1

Closed Social Dance Position

Plate 2
Open Social Dance Position, Outside Hands on Hips

Plate 3

Open Social Dance Position, Outside Hands Joined and Extended Forward

Plate 4
Partners Side by Side, Inside Hands Joined at Shoulder Level

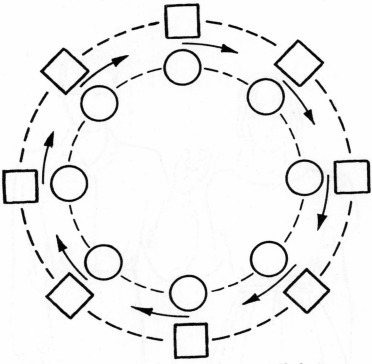

Diagram 1—Double Circle, Facing Clockwise

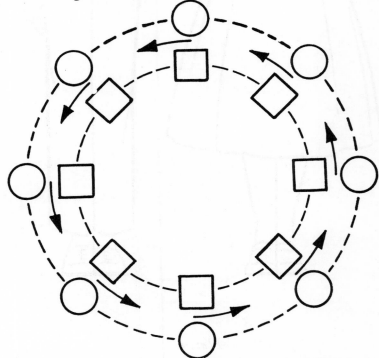

Diagram 2—Double Circle, Facing Counterclockwise

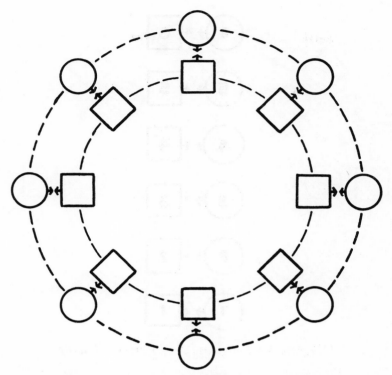

Diagram 3 — Double Circle, Partners Facing

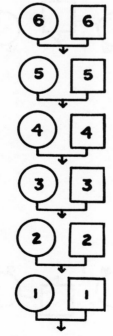

Diagram 4 — Longways Set, Facing Up

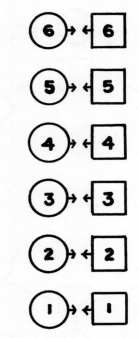

Diagram 5 — Longways Set, Partners Facing

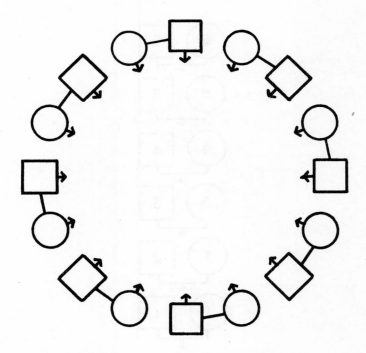

Diagram 6 — Single Circle, Facing In

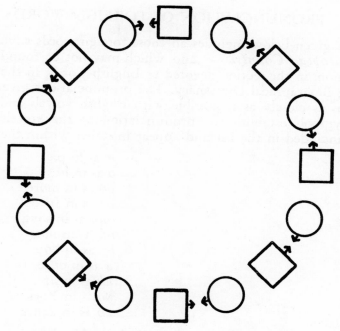

Diagram 7 — Single Circle, Partners Facing

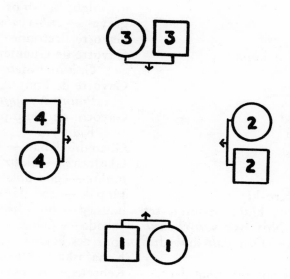

Diagram 8 — Quadrille or Square Formation

PRONUNCIATION OF FOREIGN WORDS

The list of words given below includes all those foreign words which appear in this volume — *Folk Dances of European Countries* — and which may not be found in *Webster's Collegiate Dictionary*, Fifth Edition, in the section devoted to English words, in the Pronouncing Gazeteer, or in the Pronouncing Biographical Dictionary. The pronunciations given here approximate the foreign pronunciations as closely as is possible with English vowels and consonants.

The following symbols establish the pronunciation of the vowels and consonant sounds in the various words included in the list and appear in italics within the syllables of each word:

a as in t*a*g
ah as in f*a*ther
ain as in br*an*ch
aun as in h*aun*t
e as in m*e*t
ea as in *ea*rn
ee as in p*ee*k
eh as in p*ay*
ei as in th*ey*'re
g as in *g*et
i as in h*i*t

ie as in p*ie*
o as in l*o*ss
oh as in m*o*re
oo as in f*oo*d
oun as in s*o*ng
ow as in n*ow*
oy as in b*oy*
u as in c*u*re
uh as in *u*p
yo as in *Y*ork
zh as in a*z*ure

Alemanni — *Ah-leh-máhn-ee*
Arkon — *Ahr-kon*
Báboushka — *Báh-boosh-kah*
badnyak — *báhd-nee-ack*
balaláika — *bah-lah-lie-kah*
Bandltanz — *Báhn-d'l-tahnts*
Barina — *Bah-ree-nah*
Bergkulbi — *Béirk-kool-bee*
binjou — *bain-zhoo*
bourée — *boo-reh*
branle, branles — *braunl*
Branle Gascon — *Braunl Gas-koun*
bubën — *boob-yon*
Burgundii — *Boor-góon-dee-ee*
Chiemgau — *Héem-gow*
Chrovod — *Khoh-roh-vohd*
cimbalom — *tsím-bah-lom*
Csárdá — *Chár-da*
Csárdás — *Chár-dahsh*
Csébogar — *Chéh-boh-gar*
Čtyři Kroky — *Chti-rshi Kro-ki*
Der Haxenschmeiszer — *Deir Háhks'n-shmié-ser*
Der Neubavarische — *Deir Nóy-báh-vah-ri-shuh*
Der Paschade Flügs-Ummi — *Deir Pah-sháh-duh Flóoks-óo-mee*
Der Strohschneider — *Deir Shtróh-shnie-der*
domra — *dóm-rah*

duda — *dóo-dah*
dúdka — *dóot-kah*
écossaise — *eh-ko-sez*
Edate — *Eh-dat*
Fête des Rois — *Fet deh Rwah*
Fête Dieu — *Fet Dyea*
Fête Nationale — *Fet Na-syo-nal*
Freut euch des Lebens — *Froyt oykh dehs Léh-b'ns*
gatyas — *gúh-tyahsh*
Gavotte Bretonne — *Ga-vot Bre-ton*
Gavotte de Guéméné — *Ga-vot duh Geh-meh-neh*
Gavotte de Pont-Aven — *Ga-vot duh Pount-A-vaun*
Gavotte de Quimper — *Ga-vot duh Kain-pér*
Ghenghis Khán — *Chyen-ghees-Kháhn*
Glasltanz — *Gláhz'l-tahnts*
gudók — *goo-dók*
Hopák — *gah-páhk*
housky — *hoos-kee*
Jabado — *Zha-ba-doh*
Jour des Fagots — *Zhoor deh Fa-goh*
Kanafaska — *Ku-nu-fu-sku*
Kehraus — *Kéir--ows*
Khevsurs — *Khev-sóors*

Kolenda — Ko-len-dah
Kolo — Ko-lo
Kolomýka — Koh-loh-meh-kah
Koróboushka — Kah-ro-boosh-kah
koulích — koo-léech
La Boudigueste — La Boo-dee-gest
Ländler — Lánt-leir
Langtanze — Láhng-tahn-tsuh
lapots — lah-póts
Lauterbach — Lów-teir-bahkh
Le Jour de l'An — Luh Zhoor duh laun
Lekuri — Leh-koo-ree
le petit Jésus — luh ptee Zheh-zu
Le Stoupic — Luh Stoo-peek
Lezghínka — Lyes-ghéen-kah
Locminé — Lók-mee-neh
Lvóv — Ljvov
Makovitza — Mah-ko-vít-tsah
Matkanje — Ma-chah-nye
Mersen — Méir-z'n
Michaél Feódorovich — Mee-khah-éel
     F-yaw-daw-raw-veech
Mois de Marie — Mwah d Mar-ee
Motovidlo — Mo-to-vi-dlo
Mühlrad — Muhl-rahd
Na Ty Louce Zeleny — Na Ti Lou-tse
     Ze-le-ni

Odzemok — Od-ze-mok
Ostern — Óhs-teirn
Pâques — Pahk
passepied — pahs-pyeh
prisjádka — pree-syáht-kah
Resnik — Rshez-neek
rigaudon — ree-go-doun
róg — rok
Róus — Róoss
Rügen — Róo-gen
Šátečková — Sha-tech-ko-vah
Schuhplattler — Shóo-plaht-leir
Sedloček — Sed-lo-chek
Šeucovská — Shoo-tsof-skah
Siebenschritt — Zée-b'n-shrit
sous — soo
Stretta — Stret-tah
Szolo — Sóh-loh
tárogató — tah-roh-guh-toh
Trihoris — Tree-or-ee
volte — volt
volýnka — vah-lin-kah
Weggis — Véh-gis
Zalman — Tsahl-mahn
Zaporozhets — Zah-pah-roh-zhyets
zhaleika — zhah-léh-kah
Zhuraval — Zhoo-rah-vel

FOLK DANCES OF SWITZERLAND AND GERMANY

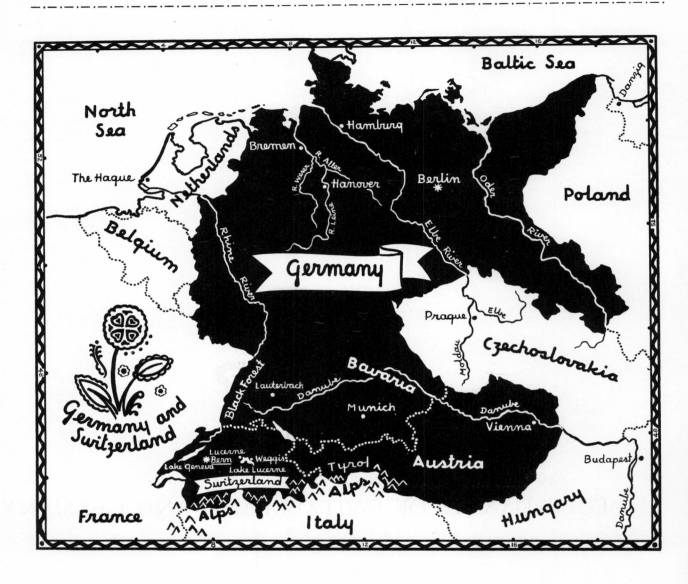

Switzerland and Germany

GEOGRAPHICAL BACKGROUND

Switzerland — Tiny Switzerland is cradled in the midst of the Alps, surrounded on all sides by other European countries. Italy lies to the south, Germany to the north and northeast, Austria to the east, and France to the west and northwest. The area of Switzerland is 15,950 square miles, slightly larger than the combined areas of Massachusetts, Connecticut, and Rhode Island.

Switzerland boasts one of the most spectacular landscapes of any country in the world. The beauty of her snow-covered mountain peaks, clear, still lakes, dense forests, and glaciers have made her famous as a country with exquisite scenery. The climate of Switzerland varies with the diverse types of topography characterizing different sections of this country. In some of the higher regions, winter continues the entire year while in the lower valleys, the seasons of spring, summer, fall, and winter rotate proportionately. The annual rainfall varies in different localities but is adequate in all sections of the country.

Because a large portion of Switzerland is mountainous, relatively few agricultural products are grown in this country. Cereal grains, potatoes, beets, and grapevines, however, are cultivated in sufficient quantities for home consumption. The chief agricultural industry is dairying. Cattle and sheep graze in the excellent pasture lands on the slopes of the mountains in summer and are brought down into the lower valleys during the winter season. The country is famous for its superior cheeses and butter.

The production of fine textiles is the chief manufacturing industry of Switzerland. This small country is famous for its cottons, silks, and laces as well as for its linens, woolens and embroideries. Another industry for which Switzerland is well known is the manufacture of fine clocks and watches which constitute the third greatest export of the country. One of the outstanding folk arts of Switzerland is exquisite woodcarving resulting in the production of singularly life-like figures which are facsimiles of peasant folk associated with this country of rich folklore. In the final analysis, however, perhaps the most important industry in Switzerland is that of entertaining thousands of annual visitors from all over the world in her numerous resorts at various seasons of each year.

Germany — With the defeat of Germany by the allied countries as a culmination of World War II in 1945, the original area of 137,674 square miles — slightly smaller in size than the state of Montana — was divided into four sections, each of which was allocated to the supervision of occupational forces representative of the United States in the southern area, England in the northwestern, France in the southwestern, and Russia in the northeastern; joint headquarters for the four separate powers were established in Berlin. The ultimate boundaries of Germany as a nation, following this period of reconstruction, must await future developments in the history of the world. The present occupied area is bounded on the south by Switzerland and Austria, on the east by Czechoslovakia and Poland, on the north by Denmark and the North and Baltic Seas, and on the west by the Netherlands, Belgium, Luxembourg, and France.

North of Switzerland are the Bavarian Alps of Southern Germany. From these mountains, the topography of Germany slopes gradually to a highland section in Central Germany and on down to the lowland regions of Northern Germany along the coast of the North Sea. There are several important rivers — the Rhine, the Weser, the Elbe, and the Danube, emptying into the North Sea and the Black Sea, and the Oder which flows into the Baltic Sea. All are navigable for a part of their respective courses and are significant for their historical, economic, and aesthetic associations. The climate in the highland region of Germany is likely to be pleasant in summer but quite severe in winter; however, those living in the river valleys enjoy a mild, pleasant climate throughout the year. Rainfall in Germany is adequate for extensive agriculture to be carried on during all seasons of the year.

Germany is both an agricultural and industrial country. The rich river beds provide fertile soils for raising crops of grain, truck, fruits, and nuts as well as pasture lands. The chief crops of Germany are wheat, rye, oats, barley, potatoes, sugar beets, vegetables, fruits — especially apples, cherries, peaches, apricots, plums, and pears — nuts, hops — used extensively throughout the country for brewing beer for which Germany is famous — grapevines, tobacco, flax, and hemp. Extensive forest regions cover Germany, especially in the mountainous section of the south. Mineral deposits include large stores of coal and iron with gold, silver, lead, zinc, and copper mined extensively in various sections of the country.

Germany's industries are primarily concerned with the conversion of her raw materials into finished products. There are large iron and steel industries in various parts of the country. Textiles — linen, cotton, woolen, and silk fabrics — are manufactured for home consumption and for export purposes. Porcelain, pottery, and glass are produced in East and South Germany and fine clocks and woodwork in the southern part of the country. In the northern part of Germany, large quantities of beet sugar are refined.

HISTORICAL AND SOCIOLOGICAL BACKGROUND

Switzerland — The original inhabitants of Switzerland known as the Helvetians were conquered by Julius Caesar and remained for four centuries under Roman domination — until 375 A.D. As the Roman Empire declined, the Alemanians, a South German tribe, drove the Romans out of Eastern Switzerland while another Germanic tribe, called the Burgundians, founded a kingdom in the western part of Switzerland. From the sixth to the ninth centuries the two groups were united as a part of the Frankish Empire. With the collapse of the empire in the ninth century, Eastern Switzerland was organized as the Duchy of Alemania (or Upper Germany) while Western Switzerland became once more the Kingdom of Burgundy. Both divisions became part of the Holy Roman (actually German) Empire in 1032.

The emperors of Germany during the Middle Ages grew less and less powerful while the nobles, who ruled the various duchies into which Germany was divided, became increasingly so. Seizing upon this opportunity for exerting influence over the people, the ruling nobility required the small towns in their realms to pay heavy taxes in return for promised protection. Three small forest districts — Uri, Schwyz, and Unterwalden — which were included in those lands near Lake Lucerne, were governed by a member of the Habsburg family of Austria. The people of these districts rebelled against the tyrannies of their ruler and formed, in 1291, an Everlasting League or "Perpetual Pact" for the purpose of defense against their mutual enemy, the Habsburgs. With the establishment of this Swiss Confederation, the inhabitants declared themselves unwilling to submit to Austrian rule or to any tyrannical form of domination. They were forced to defend their declared independence against the Austrians several times but were successful in remaining free and also in annexing, either through conquests or through the voluntary entrance of adjacent lands into the Confederation, small units of surrounding territory which were called cantons. Late in the fifteenth century the Swiss defeated Maximilian I of the Holy Roman Empire who had tried to subject them to taxation. The Swiss Confederation became virtually independent as a result of the Peace of Basle.

During the Reformation, civil war broke out within the cantons as a result of conflicts between the aristocracy and democracy as well as between Catholicism and Protestantism. One of the results of the Reformation in Switzerland was the universal recognition of the country as a center of Protestant thinking. Another significant result was the formal recognition of the independence of Switzerland by the powers of Europe in the Peace of Westphalia (1648) which closed the bloody Thirty Years War. The following century and a half saw the flourishing of the aristocratic-democratic republics, the flowering of culture, and the promotion of trade.

The local loyalties and the lack of national patriotism made the Swiss vulnerable to foreign aggression. In 1798, with the occupation of Switzerland by French troops following the French Revolution, Switzerland was reorganized to form the Helvetic Republic which lasted only four years. In 1803, under the Act of Mediation, Napoleon organized the country into a new confederation composed of nineteen cantons. One of the chief problems which Switzerland faced was that of neutrality deemed essential by this small country wedged in between more powerful nations which might become hostile. This newly organized state was recognized by the Congress of Vienna in 1815, one of the acts of the Congress assured the neutrality of Switzerland in future wars. Throughout the following century Switzerland has continued to advance socially, politically, and economically. Of special interest to Americans is the Swiss Constitution of 1848 which is based on the United States Constitution.

During both World Wars I and II, Switzerland successfully maintained her state of neutrality despite the fact that it was often a struggle for her to do so. As a neutral nation, Switzerland faced was that of neutrality deemed essential by this small country wedged in between more powerful nations which might become hostile. This newly organized state was recognized by the Congress of Vienna in 1815; one of the acts of the Congress assured rulers who found themselves without a country. Through her neutrality, Switzerland was able to perform services which spared various peoples of the world much suffering and hardship.

Since 1874 Switzerland has been a federated republic composed of twenty-two cantons. The country is governed by the Federal Assembly which is made up of two chambers—the Council of States with two representatives from each state, and the National Council with one hundred and eighty-seven members. Members of the Federal Assembly are elected every four years by the vote of all men over twenty years of age. Every four years, the Federal Assembly elects seven men to make up the Federal Council. Each member of the Council is responsible for one of the seven Federal administrative departments. Each year, the Federal Assembly elects one of the seven members of the Council to serve as President of the Confederation and one member to serve as Vice-President of the Federal Council.

Switzerland has operated as a democracy longer than any other country in Europe. The Swiss always have taken a fierce pride in the perpetuation of their form of government. They place their faith in the democratic state rather than in individual statesmen. One author describes their attitude toward individuals in public office as one of distrust when he states that "their heroes are all dead heroes."[1] The well-known story of William Tell who refused to remove his hat as a gesture of obeisance to the symbol of the Austrian monarch—a tale believed to be purely legendary—serves to illustrate the democratic spirit which has for generations obtained in the hearts of the Swiss who as a people, representative of a diversity of races and religious creeds, are bound closely together in their common belief in democracy.

The official languages of Switzerland are German, French, Italian, and Rhaeto-Roman, or Romansh, which has been recognized recently as an official language. Rhaeto-Roman is an independent Neo-Latin language which is spoken at present by the inhabitants of the mountain regions of the upper Rhine, largely in the canton of Grisons. It has been a literary language for about a century.

The most recent census indicates that the Protestant Faith, which is Calvinistic in doctrine and Presbyterian in form, predominates in twelve of the cantons with a total of 2,230,303 members and the Roman Catholic Faith claims the majority in ten cantons with 1,666,350 pledged to this Faith. There were, at the time of the census, 17,973 Jews in Switzerland.

Intellectually, Switzerland has contributed far more than might be expected from a country of her size. Protestant religious leaders like John Calvin and Huldreich Zwingli influenced millions of men throughout Europe and America. The educational ideas of Rousseau and the modern practices of Pestalozzi were instrumental in reshaping educational methods all over the world.

Germany — The dawn of recorded history reveals the territory now known as Germany filled with roving tribes of Teutonic people, members of the same tall, blond-haired folk who roamed over Scandinavia. These early Teutons, later called Germans, were the "barbarians from the north" whom the Romans feared. When, in the course of the expansion of the Roman Empire, the Romans sought to conquer these tribes, they were defeated in the decisive battle of Teutoburg Forest in 9 A.D., thus determining for Germany a Teutonic rather than a Latin heritage. During the following eight centuries, Germany was the scene of tribal migrations and conflicts. Late in the eighth century the tribe of the Franks emerged as the most powerful Germanic group.

During the reign of Clovis as king of the Franks, many of the German tribes were incorporated in the Frankish Kingdom. When Charlemagne extended the Frankish Empire over Europe, German lands, as far east as the Elbe River, were included in his Empire. With the

---

[1]Robert Clarkson Brooks, *Civic Training in Switzerland* (Chicago: The University of Chicago Press, 1930), p. 5.

Treaty of Verdun in 843, the territory won by Charlemagne was apportioned to his grandsons. Louis "the German," was assigned dominion of the territory east of the Rhine and his half-brother, Charles "the Bald," the western section of the empire. In the later Treaty of Mersen in 870, Louis and Charles further clarified the boundaries of their kingdoms in which Germany extended east as far as the Elbe River and the Bohemian Mountains and west as far as the Rhine River, including the provinces of Alsace and Lorraine. For the first time, the tribes of Germany were under one central government composed of several duchies.

With the death of Louis the cohesiveness of the central government of Germany disintegrated leaving the country easy prey to Vikings from the north and Moravian and Magyar hordes from the east. During this period feudalism increased rapidly as it was necessary for men to attach themselves to one of the ruling dukes for protection. In 919, Henry "the Fowler," ruler of Saxony, was chosen king. He succeeded in driving out the invading armies and, by establishing a federated state, laid the foundation for the German Empire. Otto I, who succeeded Henry "the Fowler" in 936, strengthened the position of the German crown by limiting the power of the nobles, conquered Lombardy, and received from the Pope the title of Holy Roman Emperor. Conrad II, who ruled from 1024 to 1039, secured Burgundy for Germany and reduced Poland to a vassal dukedom. An outstanding feature of this period in German history was the constant struggle between the emperors and the popes.

In 1138 a new dynasty came to the imperial throne of Germany, the Hohenstaufens, whose chief purpose it was to maintain Germany's power over its people and to reduce the power of the Pope in that country. One of the Hohenstaufens, Frederick I, (Barbarossa) was the greatest ruler of the Hohenstaufen dynasty and probably would have strengthened the imperial power immeasurably had he not met his death during the Third Crusade. Frederick II, who came to the throne in 1215, was the most brilliant of the medieval German monarchs. However, he was primarily interested in the extension of the German Empire in Italy and spent most of his time and effort there. With the death of Conrad IV, successor to Frederick II in 1254, the glory of the Hohenstaufens and of the German Empire came to a close. Germany existed as an anarchy for nearly twenty years after the last Hohenstaufen and during what is called the "Great Interregnum."

In 1273 Rudolph of Habsburg was installed as king of Germany and was the first of that family of monarchs, the Habsburgs, who ruled Germany longer than any other royal line. The Golden Bull of 1356 gave Germany a form of constitution which strengthened the power of the separate duchies and kingdoms thus securing feudalism and preventing the consolidation of a unified Germany. Under the terms of the Bull, the selection of the German ruler was vested in a group of seven electors—four lords of lesser duchies and three archbishops. These powers frequently chose weak men as monarchs in order to preserve the strength of their own individual power. This lack of feeling for strong central unity, plus the frequent local wars, prevented the development of a united German kingdom for many years.

It was not until 1493, under Maximilian I of Austria, that Germany again became a unified nation. His grandson, Charles V, was even more powerful than his grandfather and brought imperial rule to its height. It was at this time that Martin Luther, a Catholic friar, began in Germany a reformation movement which ultimately became a revolution with political and social as well as religious implications. The long conflict between Catholics and Protestants was brought to a temporary end in 1555 by the Peace of Augsburg which granted the rulers of the various principalities the right to determine whether Lutheranism or Catholicism should prevail in their particular provinces.

The reigns of Charles' successors, Ferdinand, Maximilian II, and Rudolph II, saw a continuation and further growth of the movement known as the Counter-Reformation and an ever-widening breach between the Catholics and the Protestants in Germany. In 1618, the terrible struggle known as the Thirty Years War began; it ended in 1648 with the Treaty of Westphalia, leaving Germany in a state of political, economic, and social collapse. One of the German states, Prussia, was at this time becoming very powerful. The ruler of Prussia who took the title of king in 1701, Frederick William I, was to give his allegiance to the Emperor of the Holy Roman Empire who was, as well, the Emperor of Austria. There was, however, growing antagonism between Prussia and Austria and little cooperation between these two German states. The death of Emperor Charles VI brought to an end the male line of Habsburg rulers in Austria, and his daughter, Maria Theresa, became ruler of the Habsburg lands of Austria. Soon afterwards, Frederick II of Prussia attempted to claim Silesia and thereby engaged Austria in the Silesian Wars which culminated in Prussia's victory, the gain of Silesia for Prussia, and the establishment of Frederick II, or Frederick "the Great," as a brilliant military leader. Tension between Austria and Prussia continued. In 1756, Prussia went to war against Austria, Saxony, France, and Russia. Her sole ally was England who gave aid only in terms of funds. Because of Frederick's leadership, Prussia was victorious in 1763, bringing to an end the Seven Years' War which had served to strengthen Prussia and to increase the hatred between Prussia and Austria.

The new ideas of government born in the French Revolution were diametrically opposed to the absolute form of German government and resulted in a declaration of war on the part of France against Prussia and Austria in 1792. The Germans were forced to abandon the war with France in 1794 in order to save Poland from Russia. As a result of this conflict, France regained her possession of Alsace and Lorraine.

In 1800, Napoleon began the conquest of Europe and by 1807 had conquered Austria, establishing in its place the Confederation of the Rhine, had occupied Prussia, and had destroyed the Holy Roman Empire. Following Napoleon's defeat and the settlement of European affairs in 1815 by the Congress of Vienna, Prussia and Austria regained most of their former territory.

About the middle of the nineteenth century, the first German political parties arose, agitating for individual liberties and rights protected by effective and unified government. The agitation soon became a real revolution. Frederick William IV refused the demands of his subjects until the revolution flared up in Berlin when, realizing the proportions of national feeling, he called the Frankfurt Parliament for the purpose of unifying Germany. However, neither Prussia nor Austria recognized the work of the Parliament and Frederick William IV refused the crown as emperor of the united Germany; the Parliament, therefore, failed in its mission.

In 1861 a new king, William I, came to the throne of Prussia with Bismarck, one of the outstanding nation-builders of all time, as the real governing spirit behind the throne. Prussia and Austria became involved in a war with Denmark over the state of Schleswig-Holstein. After their victory in 1864, they went to war against each other over the spoils of the Danish War with the result that Austria suffered defeat. Prussia's power and prestige mounted with her formation of the North German Confederation which excluded Austria. The Prussians, however, had a strong enemy in France and in her Emperor, Napoleon III. A conflict over the right of a Hohenzollern candidate to the throne of Spain provided France with an opening for war with Prussia. As a result of the war, France lost the territories of Alsace and Lorraine. During this war, the intense national feeling which was awakened within the German states resulted in the proclamation of William I as Emperor of a united Germany in 1871. Bismarck resigned his position in 1890 and Germany continued to have a leading part in the various European affairs of the nineteenth and early twentieth centuries.

German policy following the assassination of Archduke Francis Ferdinand in 1914 was based upon the fact that Austria-Hungary was her one ally in Europe and must be protected even to the point of war with France and Russia. World War I followed and Germany was defeated in 1918. Two days before the armistice was signed, the German Empire fell and was replaced by the German Republic with Friedrich Ebert as its first president.

For fifteen years following the armistice, Germany existed precariously as a Federal Republic. In 1933, Adolf Hitler, leader of the powerful National Socialist Party, was accepted by President Von Hindenburg as chancellor of Germany. When President Von Hindenburg died in 1934, Hitler seized control of the entire government and decreed himself both President and Chancellor of Germany and established a centralized totalitarian state. Ignoring the provision of the Treaty of Versailles, Hitler rearmed Germany and, in 1939, he began a campaign of aggression in Central Europe which precipitated World War II. Germany fought with Italy, Japan, and lesser satellites against England, France, Russia, and the United States. In 1945, she surrendered unconditionally to the Allied Powers and, at present, her territory is still divided and under military occupation and government by England, France, the United States, and Russia.

According to a census of 1939, the population of Germany was 69,459,825 citizens. The most recent religious census lists approximately sixty-two per cent of the German people as Protestant, most of whom are Lutherans, and thirty-two per cent as Roman Catholic. Four per cent are members of other religious sects and seven-tenths per cent are Jews.

Germans who are recognized and appreciated throughout the world for their cultural contributions in various fields include Kant, Schopenhauer, and Nietzsche in philosophy; Heine, Goethe, Schiller, and Mann in literature; Dürer and Holbein in art; Beethoven, Brahms, Bach, Händel, Schumann, Mendelssohn, and Wagner in music; and Koch, Ehrlich, and Röntgen in science.

FOLK DANCES

The folk dances of Switzerland and Germany, especially those of Switzerland and Bavaria, are similar in terms of formations, steps, and style or type of movements. This is due in part to the proximity of Switzerland to Southern Germany which has resulted in an interchange of their respective folk cultures and to the fact that, geographically, these countries share comparable climates and topography.

Records of the early dances of Switzerland and Germany show a similarity as to general theme, formation, and movement to the dances of the same period in other European countries. Ceremonial sword dances were performed in the traditional circular formation and involved at some point the interlacing of swords to form definite designs. Sachs tells of a sword dance from Westphalia in which the leader of the group jumped upon the interlaced swords of the dancers and was tossed by them up to the crossbeams of the house where he remained for a subsequent portion of the dance itself. When the swords were again locked together, he let himself down onto them.[1] The dance about a pole, which historians believe to be an outgrowth of the dancing about a sacred tree in pagan spring fertility rites, is common to many countries all over the world. The *Bandltanz* of Southern Bavaria involves dancing about a pole to which are attached many-colored ribbons. These are twisted and braided during the course of the dance, a feature of the traditional Maypole dances performed on May Day in many countries.[2] The *Glasltanz*, a German dance from the Middle Ages in which the leader danced with a glass of water on his head, illustrates dances purported to demonstrate the prowess of an individual performer.[3] The *Schuhplattler*, when danced by two men as a mock fight between two male birds, also demonstrates prowess and agility in leaping and in the intricate clapping and slapping movements involved in its performance. The limping movement found in the dances of many countries at some point in the development of this particular aspect of their folk cultures is included in the *Chiemgau*, performed in the southern part of Bavaria. It is a marriage dance in which the bride limps. According to ancient folklore, the limp symbolizes her incomplete personality. The complete development of personality occurs only upon her transition into a new existence in marriage.[4]

The most spectacular of the early folk dances of this particular region is the *Schuhplattler* as a couple dance which includes the *ländler* as one part of its performance. This *Schuhplattler*, a courtship dance, dramatizes the wooing of the woman by the man. The woman spins demurely for a good portion of the dance while the man follows her in close pursuit with elaborate slapping and clapping movements designed to attract her attention. Finally, the couple dance together in the turning *ländler*, and the climax comes when the man tosses his partner high into the air and brings her gently down again at his side. The last movement is executed only by the stoutest dancers who have sufficient strength left for it at the finish of the dance.

Certain typical folk dance formations common to many countries are found in Swiss and German dances. The chain or choral dance, with the performers in a long line, is the design for the German *Kehraus*[5] and *Langtanze*[6] and for the Swiss *Allewander*.[7] The arrangement of the dancers in sets comprised of two women and one man is the basic formation for

---

[1]Curt Sachs, *World History of the Dance* (New York: W. W. Norton Company, 1937), p. 120.
[2]*Ibid.*, p. 65.
[3]*Ibid.*, p. 221.
[4]*Ibid.*, p. 130.   [6]*Ibid.*, p. 151.
[5]*Ibid.*, p. 272.   [7]*Ibid.*, p. 163.

Come, Let Us Be Joyful, a German folk dance included in this collection. The *bunt* dances, most popular in Northern Germany, are performed usually by eight people in quadrille formation. In the course of the dance, several figures are described while the dancers move with a strongly accented walking step.[1] Basic patterns of movement and designs are readily recognized as precursors of our American square dances.

Throughout Germany and Switzerland, perhaps the most popular folk dances are the couple dances—the waltz, the polka, and the schottische. The waltz—a familiar dance form descended from the peasant *ländler*, an earlier dance form in Germany—is synonymous with German dance, especially in Southern Germany. The musical background for the waltzes of Switzerland and Germany is frequently hearty and gay, though often it is particularly charming with a light, tinkling quality suggestive of delicate mountain crocuses or edelweiss, the sound of music boxes manufactured in this country, or that of sheep bells. The peasant waltzes inspired Johann Strauss to write music in this form and thus, in turn, he immortalized the waltz with his beloved music. Some say that the polka comes from Bohemia but, by the middle of the nineteenth century, it had spread throughout Europe and had become a popular dance form included in social celebrations in many countries. This dance step forms the basis for many simple, though charming, German and Swiss folk dances. The schottische is said to be a variation of the waltz[2] and is the basic step of many folk dances of these countries although it does not merit the popularity of the polka and the waltz.

The dances never lack musical accompaniment because the people of these countries are known to be innately musical. In the Alpine regions, a particular stringed instrument, the zither, is used for dance accompaniment along with various types of horns. In any village, there are enough musicians to provide a band, an orchestra, or a semblance of either. There is always the possibility of singing the accompaniment for dancing since many of the folk dances of this region still retain their original musical settings of definite and significant words to established folk melodies.

FOLK COSTUMES

The traditional folk costumes worn by the people of Switzerland and Germany for festival occasions are particularly picturesque and gay. In these countries many different versions of traditional costumes appear, varying according to the provinces in which they are worn. There is relatively little difference, however, in the daily garb of the working classes. The woman wears a full skirt, a blouse with long sleeves, an apron, and a scarf on the head for outdoor chores; and the man wears a shirt, dark trousers and jacket, heavy boots, and a cap or soft hat. In the metropolitan cities, the dress for both men and women is similar to that seen in London, Paris, or New York.

Today in some sections of Switzerland, the bright costumes often are replaced with black silk or taffeta dresses and large-crowned hats for Sunday and festival wear.[3] The women in

---

[1]Elizabeth Burchenal, *Folk Dances of Germany* (New York: G. Schirmer, Inc., 1938), p. 39.
[2]Sachs, *op. cit.*, p. 432.
[3]Kathleen A. Mann, *Peasant Costumes in Europe* (London: Black, Ltd., 1931), p. 54.

other sections, however, still retain the attractive white blouse with puffed sleeves to the elbow, the black corset or bodice laced with ribbons, and the full and colorful skirt over which is worn a lovely apron. An interesting custom of the Swiss woman is the wearing of silver chains, rosettes, and various kinds of jewelry to decorate the bodice. The hats of the women vary according to particular provinces from large flat straws decorated with ribbons to small black velvet caps with a ruffle of white starched lace or woven horsehair which frames the face. Frequently, instead of wearing any headdress, young women of Switzerland entwine colored ribbons through their hair.[1]

The relatively simple costume of the men of Switzerland usually consists of a white linen shirt with either short or long sleeves; rather full, knee-length trousers; a colored waistcoat which is usually red; a dark jacket or coat; rough linen stockings and black shoes; and dark skull-caps or soft hats with brims.[2] The hat, usually worn at a very jaunty angle, sometimes has a bit of color supplied by flowers or feathers attached to the band. The men in certain sections of the country wear toboggan caps similar to those worn in Scandinavia.

An important feature of the German woman's costume is her blouse. A variety of sleeve designs prevails in the folk costumes of this country. In some sections, women wear elaborately embroidered blouses with puffed sleeves while in other places the blouses are less elaborate, with perhaps wide ruffles around the wrists of the sleeves. In general, however, the German woman wears a white blouse under a bodice of varying colors and designs, a very full skirt, a colorful apron, white woolen stockings, and black slippers. The headdress of the German woman varies, again, according to the section in which she lives. Some of the characteristic hats are large, with wide brims; others are small and decorated with a bow of ample size in the back. Many women tie a plain kerchief around the head—a very popular and simple form of headdress.

The German man's costume is similar to the one worn by men of Switzerland. Here again one finds the knee-length, varicolored trousers, though not full like those worn in Switzerland. An elaborately embroidered shirt worn under a heavy jumper or jacket, white woolen hose, and either black boots or slippers comprise a costume frequently seen. The hats worn by the Germans are comparable to those worn in Switzerland. The Bavarian men wear short, leather breeches, a white shirt, embroidered suspenders, heavy shoes, divided, ribbed woolen socks, and a cap accented with a feather or flower.

FOLK FESTIVALS

Because of the religious differences among the various peoples of Switzerland and Germany, the celebration of feast days varies somewhat in the different sections of each of these two countries. In those regions where the Roman Catholic Church constitutes the predominate faith, religious festivals are frequent and follow the days and seasons for feasting or fasting indicated on the church calendar. The major festivals observed are quite similar and are celebrated in much the same manner.

---

[1] Mann, *op. cit.*
[2] *Ibid.*, p. 55.

Easter, known as *Ostern* in both Switzerland and Germany, is celebrated with morning church services and beautiful Easter music. The remainder of the day's celebration in Switzerland includes the hunting of Easter eggs for the children and feasting and merrymaking for the adults. The special day in Germany centers largely around the hunting of Easter eggs thought to be hidden in many strange places by the traditional rabbit. An interesting custom in Northwestern Germany is the contest held to determine who among the group can devour the largest number of eggs.[1] Various other contests such as racing for hidden eggs and rolling eggs downhill are also held in conjunction with the celebration of *Easter* in Germany.

On December 6, St. Nicholas brings Christmas goodies to children in some sections of Switzerland and of Germany. This festival, known as the *Eve of St. Nicholas*, is celebrated with a visit from a very merry fellow who calls immediately after supper to question the children of each household regarding their conduct during the preceding year. If they are able to report good behavior, and if they can recite a jingle, he rewards them with fruit and cakes and promises to see them on Christmas Eve.[2]

On *Christmas Eve* the Christ Child, rather than Santa Claus, is thought to bring toys and confections to children in certain sections of Switzerland. Swiss people celebrate the festival with the singing of carols and story-telling. An interesting superstition found in both Switzerland and Germany is the legendary belief that, in the middle of the night, the animals converse with each other using human speech. In the German Alps, it is considered a great sin to eavesdrop upon the cattle when they are conversing at midnight.[3] Another belief prompts Swiss housewives to clip the wings of their chickens between eleven and twelve midnight as a means of protection from beasts who might otherwise devour them.[4] *Christmas Day* is spent in feasting within the various homes. In Germany, the country from which comes the traditional decorated Christmas tree, a resplendent tree is on exhibition from Christmas Eve through the following day in the homes of the people. December 25 is devoted primarily to an exchange of gifts.[5]

New Year's Day, though observed in both Switzerland and Germany, is celebrated with different festivities. In Switzerland, crowds gather to observe amateur dramatic performances but otherwise the people spend a relatively quiet day. According to German peasant superstition, *New Year's Day* should be lived as one would like to live during the year following. This belief necessitates avoiding one's doctor, being very friendly to all acquaintances, and exhibiting exemplary behavior.[6]

Numerous special ceremonies and celebrations center about the chief occupations of the Swiss people. Such festivals vary according to specific sections but include *Shepherd Sunday*, the second Sunday in September, when the folk of Valais celebrate the return of the sheep

---

[1] Dorothy Spicer, *The Book of Festivals* (New York: The Womans Press, 1932), p. 134.
[2] William S. Walsh, *Curiosities of Popular Custom* (Philadelphia: J. B. Lippincott Company, 1925), pp. 750-751.
[3] *Ibid.*, p. 232.
[4] Spicer, *op. cit.*, p. 321-323.
[5] Walsh, *op. cit.*, p. 234.
[6] Spicer, *op. cit.*, p. 131.

herders and their flocks from the pastures up in the Alps;[1] a *Shooting Festival* each October in Thun, when men shoot arrows at a target in the likeness of a former Austrian oppressor;[2] and the *Midsummer Feast*, or *Bergkulbi*. For the *Feast* families climb up to the pasturelands to join the men folk who have been with the flocks. There they spend the day singing, yodeling, dancing, playing games, and enjoying simple food — the fresh milk, butter, and cheese made by the men and the bread brought by the families.[3]

A particularly charming folk custom of the Swiss people celebrates the annual departure of the shepherds and the herds of milch cows from the valleys each spring when the snow has melted sufficiently to permit passage to the grassy land up in the Alpine regions. The festive herdsmen come in their red vests, dark pants, and white shirts. The lead cow wears flowers and garlands of greenery about her horns and a fancy bell about her neck. The townspeople accompany the colorful procession for a part of the way, singing and bidding the herdsmen a good season. The shepherds drive their cows to an altitude of eight to ten thousand feet. During this time, the shepherds rise early each morning to milk the cows and spend the day making cheeses and butter.[4] At sundown, the senior herdsman of one group sounds the vesper hour with the melody of a psalm played on the Alphorn, a long ten or twelve-foot horn made from a hollowed tree. The rich strange tones reach out to the surrounding mountain peaks and are soon joined by the tones from other Alphorns — a general signal for prayer. In the lengthening shadows of the majestic Alps, with the haunting tones of the horn still in their ears, the shepherds must find the "holy time" truly a period for breathless adoration.[5]

A festival day in Switzerland is August 1 or *Independence Day* in commemoration of that date in 1291 which marked the inauguration of the Swiss Confederation. This national holiday is celebrated with fireworks, bonfires, the ringing of bells, parades, singing, and feasting.[6]

Leonard's Ride is an interesting festival observed in Germany on November 6 in memory of St. Leonard, patron saint of cattle. If November 6 does not fall upon a Sunday, custom defers the festival to the Sunday which immediately follows that date. On the day of the festival, gaily decorated wagons harnessed to powerful horses approach the church. The wagons are driven by the men of the community who, with their wives beside them, make a colorful picture in their festival attire. The cattle which have returned from the pastures are brought to the festival accompanied by the herdsmen. The Germans dress very gaily and, after attending a solemn Mass, devote the remainder of the day to dancing and singing.

A festival celebrated in Germany which corresponds to the Midsummer Eve festival of the Scandinavian countries is *Summer Solstice*. This festival, observed on the evening of June 23 commemorating the longest day of the year, features dancing, marching, and singing by the young people followed by the building of St. John's fire. All dance around the fire and many leap through the flames to exhibit their courage and agility.[7]

---

[1]Spicer, *op. cit.*, pg. 320.
[2]*Ibid.*, p. 321.
[3]Douglas Ashby, *Things Seen in Switzerland in Summer* (London: Seeley, Service and Co., Ltd., 1928), p. 31.
[4]*Ibid.*, p. 28.
[5]*Ibid.*, p. 30.
[6]Spicer, *op. cit.*, p. 320.
[7]*Ibid.*, p. 136-137.

SWISS SCHOTTISCHE

This is an excellent "mixer" for a folk dance party because of its progressive change of partners with each repetition of the two-part form analyzed. Due to this feature of the dance, it is called both "The Swiss Changing Polka" and "The Swiss Changing Dance." The former is something of a misnomer, however, as the dance is really a schottische, combining the running schottische step and step-hops used basically in the schottisches of various countries.

Formation: Any number of couples in a double circle facing counterclockwise, Man on L of partner, hands on hips.

	COUNTS	MEASURES
A. Beginning on outside feet (Man L, Woman R), partners separate, dancing sideward away from each other (Man moving to L, Woman R), with		
1 running schottische step	1&,2&	1
Beginning on inside feet, partners dance sideward toward each other (Man moving to R, Woman L) with		
1 running schottische step	1&,2&	2

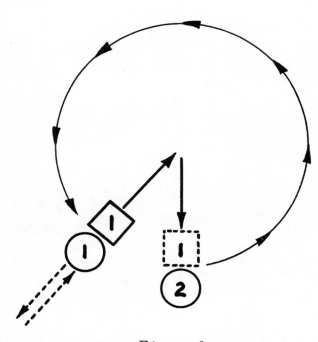

Diagram 9

	COUNTS	MEASURES
B. In shoulder-waist position, partners make two turns clockwise in place with		
4 step-hops (Man L, R, L, R, Woman R, L, R, L) finishing side by side in original starting position		3-4

COUNTS MEASURES

Repeat A except that Man, instead of returning to his partner with the second running schottische step, progresses diagonally forward R in order to dance B with the next Woman in the counterclockwise circle ahead of his partner. [See Diagram 9, page 45] .   5-6

Repeat B with new partners   7-8

Repeat All   9-16

Repeat entire dance as many times as desired. If the circle is not too large, the dance is repeated until men have progressed counterclockwise around the circle to their original partners.

SWISS SCHOTTISCHE

M.M. ♪= 152   *Switzerland*

LAUTERBACH

Lauterbach is a delightful Swiss couple dance, taking its name and origin from a specific section in the southern part of Germany near the Swiss border. *Lauterbach* is the name of both a river and a town in the province of Wurttemberg, Germany. It is interesting to note that the musical accompaniment for this popular folk dance is known in this country as "Where, Oh Where, Has My Little Dog Gone" and in Germany as "I Lost My Stocking in Lauterbach."

Some of the charm of this particular folk dance in two-part form lies in the fact that changing step patterns introduce changing secondary rhythmic patterns in Figure I in contrast to the light, continuous waltz in Figure II.

Formation: Any number of couples in a large double circle, partners facing, Man's back toward center of circle, Woman's L hand in Man's R, free hands on hips, fingers toward front.

I

	COUNTS	MEASURES
A. Couples dance in place (Man beginning L, Woman R), with		
1 waltz balance step, turning away from each other and swinging joined hands strongly forward	1,2,3	1
1 waltz balance step, turning toward each other, and swinging joined hands strongly backward	1,2,3	2
Swinging joined hands strongly forward and upward, partners release hands and turn away from each other, making one complete turn progressing counterclockwise around the circle, finishing to face again [See Plate 5, page 49] with		
2 waltz steps (Man L, R, Woman R, L) except that the weight is not taken on the outside foot at the close of the second waltz step (Ct. 3, Meas. 4) to leave that foot free for repeating A . .		3-4
Repeat Meas. 1-4 reversing feet and direction, beginning on the outside foot (Man R, Woman L) and moving clockwise . . .		5-8
B. Partners facing in a double circle, Man's back to center of circle, both hands joined with arms extended sideward at shoulder level. (Man's part is analyzed; Woman's is opposite with a reversal of feet and directions throughout.) Dancers		
Step L to side	1	
Hold	2	
Close R to L, taking weight	3	1
Step L to side	1	
Hold, drawing R to L without weight	2,3	2
Repeat, moving clockwise and beginning R		3-4
Keeping both hands joined, dancers turn away from each other as in "wringing the dishrag," (Man turning under his L arm, Woman under her R arm), progressing counterclockwise, with		
2 waltz steps (Man beginning L, Woman R)		5-6

		COUNTS	MEASURES
Partners facing, arms still extended sideward			
Stamp L		1	
Hold		2	
Stamp R		&	
Stamp L		3	7
Stamp R		1	
Hold		2,3	8

C. In shoulder-waist position, couples turn clockwise while progressing counterclockwise around the large circle, with

16 waltz steps (Man beginning L, Woman R)   9-24

II

A. Repeat A of Figure I   1-8

B. Repeat B of Figure I   1-8

C. Partners facing in single circle (Man facing counterclockwise, Woman clockwise), R hands joined high, L hands on hips, couples progress counterclockwise with

16 waltz steps, Woman turning clockwise under the arch formed by the joined arms on each waltz step, Man accenting first beat of each waltz step with a stamp   9-24

Repeat entire dance as many times as desired.

Plate 5

Lauterbach

49

LAUTERBACH

Switzerland

M.M. ♩ = 144

WEGGIS DANCE

This is a favorite singing dance of the Swiss people. It takes its name from a town in Switzerland and commemorates, in a sense, one of the favorite cross-country treks in which the Swiss people engage. This route between the two villages of Lucerne and Weggis extends around the northern shores of Lake Lucerne, a fact which gives significance to the words sung in the performance of the dance. When the Swiss sing the "Hol—di—ri—dia, *et cetera*" part, the talented men yodel the phrase. Their voices soar high up the scale, the clear sounds reaching to the snow-covered mountain peaks near-by and resounding in melodious echoes.

Throughout the dance, the A part is light and quiet with something of a gentle or delicate quality whereas the B part bursts out with a vigorous, lusty quality. There is a two-measure interlude between each figure during which couples assume the starting position for dancing the next figure, using the entire phrase to make each change of position.

"Weggis Song" appears without directions for dancing in numerous collections of folk songs. It is variously titled "A Swiss Walking Song," "Weggis Song," *et cetera*. The words differ slightly in different collections but all commemorate some aspect of the cross-country walk, thereby corroborating the origin of this popular Swiss folk dance. Familiar words to three verses with a recurring refrain appear below. The words to the verses should be sung with the performance of the A part of the dance. For Figures IV and V of the dance, any of the three verses given here may be repeated or dancers may learn additional verses from other sources.

I.

A. From Lucerne to Weggis on,
   Hol di ri dia, hol di ria;
   Shoes nor stockings need we don,
   Hol di ri dia, hol dia.

B. Chorus
   Hol di ri dia,
   Hol di ri dia, hol di ria;
   Hol di ri dia,
   Hol di ri dia, hol dia.

II.

A. On the lake we all shall go,
   Hol di ri dia, hol di ria;
   See the pretty fish below,
   Hol di ri dia, hol dia.

B. Chorus

III.

A. Weggis starts the highest hill,
   Hol di ri dia, hol di ria;
   Boys and girls cheer with a will,
   Hol di ri dia, hol dia.

B. Chorus

51

Formation: Any number of couples in a double circle facing counterclockwise, Man on L of partner, hands joined in skater's grasp. [For position of hands see Swiss couple, upper right hand corner of Swiss and German Costume Plate.]

Introduction

	COUNTS	MEASURES
Hold starting position		17-18

I

A. Beginning L, couples progress forward counterclockwise around the circle with

	COUNTS	MEASURES
Touch L heel forward to floor	1	
Touch L toe to floor in front of R foot, L knee bent	2	1
1 polka step forward, beginning with a very slight hop R . .	ah 1&2	
Hold	&	2
Repeat 3 times, alternating R, L, R. Women do not take weight at end of last polka step, leaving R foot free to begin B . . .		3-8

B. With hands on hips, partners separate, Man moving diagonally forward L toward center of circle, Woman moving diagonally forward R away from the circle, turning slightly away from each other but looking back over inside shoulder at partner, with (Man's part is analyzed; Woman's is opposite with a reversal of feet and directions throughout.)

	COUNTS	MEASURES
Step L to side	1	
Close R to L, taking weight	&	
Step L to side	2	
Hop L, raising R foot slightly in back of L, R knee bent . .	&	9
Repeat, beginning R and moving diagonally forward R to return to partner [See Diagram 10]	1&,2&	10

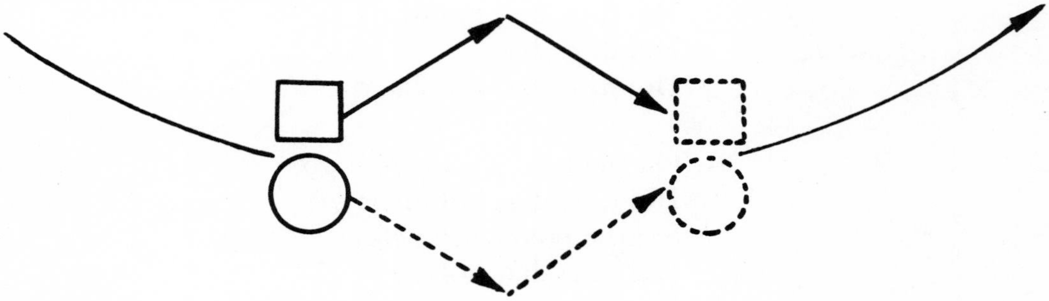

Diagram 10

Partners facing in shoulder-waist position, couples make two turns clockwise while progressing counterclockwise around the circle with

	COUNTS	MEASURES
4 step-hops (Man beginning L, Woman R)	1&,2&, 1&,2&	11-12
Repeat all		13-16

COUNTS   MEASURES

Interlude: Couples form a single circle, partners facing, Man counterclockwise, Woman clockwise. Both hands are joined with arms extended sideward (clasped hands inside the circle are lowered slightly, hands outside the circle are curved slightly overhead). [See Plate 6, page 54] .

17–18

II

A. Couples dance the heel and toe polka (as in A of Step I) moving sideward toward the center of the circle and out again (Man beginning L, Woman R), alternately dancing toward and away from the center of the circle, reversing feet and positions of clasped hands with each change of direction 1-8

B. Repeat B of Figure I 9-16

Interlude: Couples form a double circle, facing counterclockwise, hands joined in skater's grasp, weight R 17-18

III

A. Couples dance in place, all beginning L, with
    Step L to side . . . . 1&
    Point R across in front of L . . . . 2&   1
    Step R to side . . . . 1&
    Point L across in front of R . . . . 2&   2
    Couples move forward counterclockwise around the circle with
    2 polka steps, beginning with a very slight hop R, then L . . ah 1&2,   3-4
    etc.

    Repeat all. Women do not take weight at end of last polka step, leaving R foot free to begin B 5-8

B. Repeat B of Figure I 9-16

Interlude: Couples form a double circle, partners facing with Man's back to center, R hands joined high, L hands on hips 17-18

IV

A. Couples dance in place, all beginning L, with
    Step L to side . . . . 1&
    Point R across in front of L . . . . 2&   1
    Step R to side . . . . 1&
    Point L across in front of R . . . . 2&   2
    Partners exchange places moving clockwise in a half-circle [See Swiss Couple in center of Swiss and German Costume Plate] with
    2 polka steps, beginning with a slight hop R, then L . . . ah 1&2,   3-4
    etc.

    Repeat A, returning to original positions in circle.
    Women free R foot at finish to dance B 5-8

B. Repeat B of Figure I 9-16

Interlude: Couples form a double circle, partners facing, Man's back toward center of circle, Man's R hand and Woman's L hand clasped with arms extended sideward, shoulder level, away from line of direction, free hands on hips 17-18

Plate 6

Weggis Dance

V

	COUNTS	MEASURES
A. Swinging joined hands strongly forward and upward, partners release hands and turn away from each other, making one complete turn progressing counterclockwise around the circle, finishing to face again, [See Plate 5, page 49] with		
2 step-hops, (Man L, R, Woman R, L)	1&,2&	1
Step sideward (Man L, Woman R), partners join hands (Woman's R in Man's L), placing free hands on hips	1&	
Man bows, bringing feet together; Woman curtseys, placing toe of L foot slightly behind R	2	
Hold	&	2
Repeat movements analyzed for Meas. 1-2, reversing feet and directions to move clockwise around circle		3-4
Repeat all		5-8
B. Repeat B of Figure I		9-16

WEGGIS DANCE

Switzerland

SEVEN STEPS

This is one of the oldest and most widely known German dances, deriving its name from its German title, *Siebenschritt*, which means "Seven Steps," and is so called because seven running steps forward and backward constitute the A part of the dance itself.

A simple two-part form, *Seven Steps* is not only a popular dance in Germany but appears, with certain variations and under different titles, as a popular folk dance in many other countries as well, including Norway, Finland, Estonia, Czechoslovakia, and Switzerland. *Seven Steps* as danced in Germany is said to have originated in the Steiermark, Tyrol region of that country.

Either the German words or their English translation should be sung to add zest to the performance of the dance. Both are given below, keyed to the A and B parts of *Seven Steps*. They are suggestive of the migration to this country of many of our neighbors from overseas.

German	*English*
A. Ein, zwei, drei, vier, fünf, sechs, sieb'n,	A. One, two, three, four, five, six, seven,
Wo ist denn mein Schatz geblieb'n?	Where is then my sweetheart gone?
B. Ist nicht hier, ist nicht da,	B. Is not here, is not there,
Ist wohl in Amerika.	Must be in America.
Ist nicht hier, ist nicht da,	Is not here, is not there,
Ist wohl in Amerika.	Must be in America.

Formation: Any number of couples in a double circle facing counterclockwise, Man on L of partner, inside hands joined at shoulder level, outside hands on hips, fingers to the front.

	COUNTS	MEASURES
A. Partners dance forward (Man beginning L, Woman R), with 7 running steps	1&,2&, 1&,2	
Hold	&	1-2
Repeat, dancing backward to original places in circle, (Man beginning R, Woman L)		3-4
B. Releasing inside hands and placing both hands on hips, partners separate and dance away from each other (Man to L, beginning L, Woman to R, beginning R) with 3 running steps	1&,2	
Hold	&	5
Repeat, returning to partner at original position in circle (Man beginning R, Woman L)		6
In shoulder-waist position or with both hands joined (Woman's R in Man's L and *vice versa*), couples make one clockwise turn in place with 8 running steps	1&,2&, 1&,2&	7-8
Repeat all of B, finishing side by side in original starting positions		9-12

Repeat entire dance as many times as desired.

VARIATION

A more modern version of *Seven Steps* makes it very similar to the *Swiss Schottische* or *Swiss Changing Dance* included in this collection. This version follows:

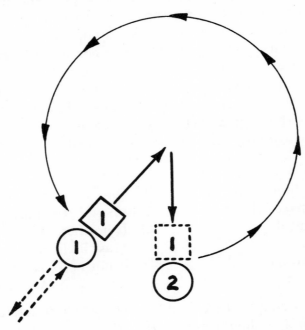

Diagram 11

	COUNTS	MEASURES
A. Formation and starting position as analyzed, couples dance forward with		
7 running steps and hold		1-2
Couples dance backward with		
7 running steps and hold		3-4
B. Releasing joined hands, Man folds his arms across chest, Woman places both hands on hips and partners dance away from each other to Man's L, Woman's R, beginning L and R, respectively, with		
1 running schottische step		5
Partners dance together again (Man beginning R, Woman L) with		
1 running schottische step		6
In shoulder-waist position, couples turn clockwise (Man beginning L, Woman R) with		
4 step-hops		7-8
Repeat all of B. Man progresses diagonally forward R on the second running schottische to the next Woman in the counterclockwise circle ahead of his partner in order to dance the step-hops with a new partner. [See Diagram 11]		9-12

Repeat entire dance as many times as desired.

SEVEN STEPS

Germany

M.M. ♪ = 152

STUPID ONE TURNING QUICKLY

This dance is known in Bavaria as *Der Paschade Flügs-Ummi* which may be translated as "The Stupid One Turning Quickly." This translation of the title injects a note of humor in its execution since the turns are taken slowly. No doubt, therefore, those who originated the dance had their tongues in their cheeks when they gave it its title.

Formation: Any number of couples in a double circle, partners facing, with Men's backs to the center of the circle, R hands joined at shoulder level, free hands on hips.

I

		COUNTS	MEASURES
A.	Couples dance in place (Man's part is analyzed; Woman's is opposite with a reversal of feet and directions throughout) with		
	Step L to side	1	
	Close R to L, taking weight	&	
	Rise on balls of feet	2	
	Lower heels	&	1
	Repeat R		2
B.	Man stands in place while Woman turns slowly clockwise under arch of joined R hands with		
	4 walking steps (R, L, R, L)	1,2,1,2	3-4
C.	Man and Woman make a quarter-turn L to join both hands back to back, arms extended sideward at shoulder level and turn clockwise in place one time with		
	4 walking steps (R, L, R, L) finishing face to face in original places at end of turn	1,2,1,2	5-6

59

	COUNTS	MEASURES
D. Stand in place and		
Clap hands to thighs	1	
Clap own hands together	2	7
Clap partner's hands 2 times (R to L and L to R)	1,2	8
Repeat A, B, C and D three times		1-8, 9-16
		9-16
		repeated

Repeat entire dance as many times as desired.

STUPID ONE TURNING QUICKLY

Bavaria

COME, LET US BE JOYFUL

This is one of the most popular German dances since it is common to many sections of that country. In Germany, it is known as *Freut euch des Lebens*, which may be translated as "Come, Let Us Be Joyful" or "Come, Let Us Be Happy." Its lilting, buoyant, and optimistic spirit is epitomized in the words which are usually sung during the execution of the dance. In characteristic fashion, many versions of the dance appear in different sections of Germany but the one recorded here is, apparently, the most prevalent. While the original text for the melody was composed by Martin Usteri in 1793, various parodies have arisen in different sections of Germany and have been recorded by Elizabeth Burchenal in her *Folk Dances of Germany*.[1] For complete satisfaction in the performance of the dance, the following words should be sung with the figures as indicated:

I.

Come, let us be joyful,
While life is bright and gay;
Gather its roses
Ere they fade away.

II.

We're always making our lives so blue,
We look for thorns and find them, too,
And leave the violets quite unseen
That on our way do grow.

III.

Repeat first stanza.

Formation: Any even number of sets of three dancers, a Man with a Woman on either side, standing side by side, inside hands joined, outside hands on hips [See group of three German dancers on Swiss and German Costume Plate], arranged in a large circle with sets of three facing alternately counterclockwise and clockwise around the circle. [See Diagram 12, page 62]

I

	COUNTS	MEASURES
All dance forward, beginning R, with 3 walking steps	1,4,1	
Men bring feet together and bow slightly *while* Women do a "bobbing curtsey," L toe in back of R heel	4	1-2
Dancers move backward to place, beginning L, with 3 walking steps	1,4,1	
Men and Women close R to L without taking weight R	4	3-4
Repeat all		5-8

---

[1] Burchenal, Elizabeth. *Folk Dances of Germany* (New York: G. Schirmer, Inc., 1938), p. 3.

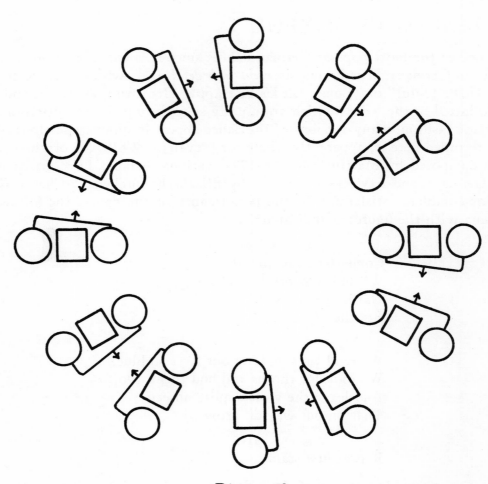

Diagram 12

II

	COUNTS	MEASURES
Man and Woman on his L hook R elbows and, beginning R, both turn clockwise once in place with		
4 skip steps	1,3,4,6, etc.	9-10
Man hooks L elbows with Woman on his R, and beginning R, both turn counterclockwise once in place with		
4 skip steps		11-12
Repeat all		13-16

III

Repeat movements as analyzed in Meas. 1-4 of Figure I		1-4
Move forward with		
4 walking steps		5-6

COUNTS   MEASURES

Releasing joined hands, continue moving forward to pass opposite
dancer by R shoulder, saluting with a slight nod of the head in passing,
with

    4 short walking steps, facing new set of 3 dancers and immedi-
    ately joining inside hands with dancers in own set of 3 . . .   7-8

Repeat entire dance as many times as desired.

COME, LET US BE JOYFUL

Germany

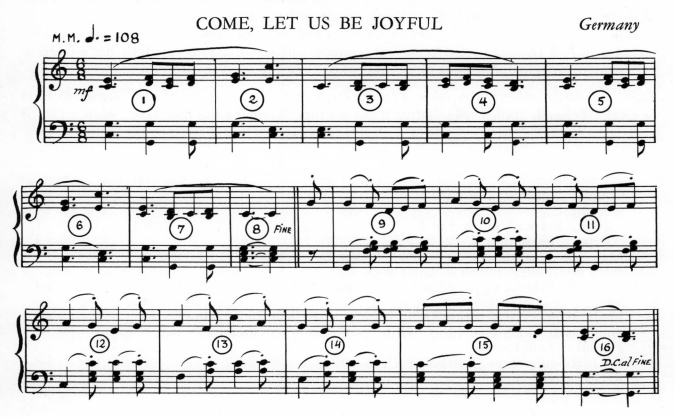

FOOT SWINGING DANCE

Foot Swinging Dance or *Der Haxenschmeiszer* is a popular folk dance among the Bavarians in the Tyrol region of Germany, taking its name from its characteristic introductory step. Its use of the pivot-turn step as well as its combination of basic steps throughout, is suggestive of certain similarities between the Bavarian dances and those of various Scandinavian countries included in *Folk Dances of Scandinavia*.[1] This simple folk dance in two-part form has a whimsical appeal in its changing dynamics which should be regarded in its performance.

Formation: Any number of couples in a double circle, partners facing, Man's back toward center of circle, R hands joined, Man's free hand on hip, Woman's holding skirt. Man's part is analyzed; Woman's part is opposite with a reversal of feet and directions throughout.

I

		COUNTS	MEASURES
A.	Couples dance in place with		
	Stamp L	1	
	Swing R across in front of L	2,3	1
	Repeat, beginning R		2
	Man dances in place *while* Woman makes two complete clockwise turns under their joined R hands with		
	2 waltz balance steps (Man L, R, Woman R, L)	1,2,3, etc.	3-4
B.	In shoulder-waist position (Man beginning L, Woman R), couples make two clockwise turns while progressing counterclockwise around the circle with		
	4 pivot-turn steps (1 step to each measure)		5-8
	Repeat A and B		1-8 2nd ending

II

	COUNTS	MEASURES
Retaining shoulder-waist position (Man beginning L, Woman R), couples make eight turns clockwise while progressing counterclockwise around the circle with		
16 waltz steps		9-16 9-16 2nd ending

Repeat entire dance as many times as desired. The *Foot Swinging Dance* may also be danced with couples arranged informally about the room rather than in a circle.

---

[1]Duggan, Anne Schley, *et al. Folk Dances of Scandinavia* (New York: The Ronald Press Company, 1948)

FOOT SWINGING DANCE

Bavaria

THE NEW BAVARIAN

Der Neubavarische or *The New Bavarian* is the German title for this simple and characteristic dance of the Bavarian Alpine region. Just what the word *new* in the Anglicized title connotes is a matter of conjecture. At any rate, it is a traditional folk dance in two-part form with basic steps which characterize many of the dances of this region—Bavarian, Swiss, German, *et cetera*—and with steps quite similar to those of Scandinavian countries.

Formation: Any number of couples in a double circle facing counterclockwise, Man on L of partner, inside hands joined, outside hands on hips.

I

		COUNTS	MEASURES
A.	Swinging joined hands forward and upward, dance 1 waltz balance step sideward away from partner (Man beginning L, Woman R)	1,2,3	1
	Swinging joined hands backward and upward, dance 1 waltz balance step sideward toward partner (Man R, Woman L).	1,2,3	2
	Standing in place, looking at partner		
	Hold, releasing joined hands	1,2	
	Clap own hands together	3	3
	Repeat clap of hands	1	
	Hold	2,3	4
	Repeat all, substituting two stamps (Man L, R, Woman R, L) for two claps		1-4 2nd ending
B.	Keeping inside hands joined, outside hands on hips, couples progress counterclockwise in a large single circle, Man moving forward in line of direction while Woman makes two counterclockwise turns (turning toward her L) under arch of joined hands, with		
	4 waltz steps (Man beginning L, Woman R)	1,2,3, etc.	5-8
	Repeat first part of A, using hand claps as before		9-12

II

In shoulder-waist position (Man beginning L, Woman R), couples turn clockwise while progressing counterclockwise around the circle with

		MEASURES
	16 waltz steps	13-20
		13-20 2nd ending

The entire dance may be repeated as many times as desired. *The New Bavarian* may also be danced with couples arranged informally about the room rather than in a large circle.

THE NEW BAVARIAN

Bavaria

THE STRAW CUTTER

The title of this simple Bavarian dance, known in that country as *Der Strohschneider*, is suggestive of its origin as an occupational dance and its proper classification in this category of folk dances with a thematic source common to many national groups. Like a number of other occupational dances, however, the movements themselves have lost their original significance.

A two-part form, *The Straw Cutter* is danced vigorously and with spirit. It is interesting to note the similarity between the step pattern of Figure I and that of the first figure in *La Virgencita*, a Mexican dance included in *Folk Dances of the United States and Mexico*.[1]

Formation: Any number of couples with partners facing in a double circle, Man's back to the center of the circle, hands joined in crossed-arm position, R arms on top of L.

I

	COUNTS	MEASURES
Couples dance in place with		
Spring to L foot, extending R foot forward, toes touching the floor	1	
Hold	&,2&	1

---

[1]Duggan, Anne Schley, *et al. Folk Dances of the United States and Mexico* (New York: The Ronald Press Company, 1948)

	COUNTS	MEASURES
Spring to R foot, extending L foot forward, toes touching the floor	1	
Hold	&,2&	2
Spring 4 times alternately to L, R, L, R, extending free foot forward to touch floor as before	1&,2&, 1&,2&	3-4
Repeat all. Woman steps L on last Ct. & of Meas. 8, freeing R foot to begin Figure II		5-8

II

In shoulder-waist position (Man beginning L, Woman R), couples make eight turns clockwise while progressing counterclockwise around the large circle with

16 pivot turn steps (2 steps to each measure)   9-16

Repeat entire dance as many times as desired. Woman finishes Figure II with weight L. To repeat dance, she hops L on Ct. 1 of Meas. 1 instead of springing to L foot. *The Straw Cutter* may also be danced with couples arranged informally about the room rather than in a circle.

THE STRAW CUTTER

Bavaria

SCHUHPLATTLER — A COUPLE DANCE

Bavaria has contributed a very old and distinctive group of folk dances known as *Schuhplattlers*, or "Shoe Clapping" dances. Because the *Schuhplattlers* are so universally danced throughout Bavaria, they may be called the national dance of that country. While there are many variations of the *Schuhplattler*, all fall into two main types—those danced by couples and those danced by two men—and all share the same characteristic feature of intriguing rhythmic patterns achieved by the men dancers through slapping the soles of their shoes and their thighs with the flat palms of their hands. The short leather breeches of the Bavarian costume afford an excellent resounding surface for the various rhythmic patterns thus produced.

The origin of the *Schuhplattler* is particularly interesting to the folklorist in that it stems ultimately from what historians would classify as animal dances of ancient times when the movements and sounds of various animals and fowls served as the thematic source for imitative dances performed by primitive man. The origin of the *Schuhplattlers* of the Tyrol region in Germany may be traced, therefore, to the strange antics of the male and female black grouse as the male woos his mate in the mountains or to the fighting movements of two male birds, similar to those seen in cock fights the world over.

The style with which the *Schuhplattler* should be danced is directly related to its origin. In both dances—the dance for a couple and the dance for two men—the man dances throughout the clapping figure with an easy up and down motion, knees relaxed, keeping his body erect—in other words, he must bring his feet and thighs up high enough to slap them without bending forward. All of his movements should be greatly exaggerated, especially the clapping and swinging of the arms which are held high overhead, fingers spread, except when they are swung far away from the body to slap the feet and thighs in imitation of the flapping of huge wings.

In the version presented below (for a man and a woman) the elaborate clapping and slapping movements of the man suggest the strutting and exhibition of the male bird in his attempts to attract the attentions of the female bird. The woman, throughout the first two parts, reacts with cool aloofness to the antics of the man, the continuous spinning suggesting the indifference shown to the male by the female bird as she preens her feathers.

In the second part of Figure II of the dance, the man is rewarded for his attentions as the woman joins him to waltz, the two dancers concluding the dance with a finish position symbolic of the woman's acceptance of the man's wooing.

In idea and general form, the spirit of this couple dance is identical with that of the *Jarabe Tapatío*, the national dance of Mexico included in *Folk Dances of the United States and Mexico*[1] in that both are courtship dances in which the man pursues the woman who is at first indifferent but eventually accepts his attentions.

Formation: Double circle facing counterclockwise, Man on L of Woman, inside hands joined, outside hands on hips, fingers to front.

---

[1]Duggan, *et al, op. cit.*

Introduction

	COUNTS	MEASURES
With joined inside hands extended slightly backward		
Step forward on outside feet (Man L, Woman R)	1	
Swing inside feet forward, swinging clasped hands downward and forward	2,3	1
Step back on inside feet	1	
Swing outside feet across in front of inside feet, swinging clasped hands backward and upward to shoulder level	2,3	2
Man twirls Woman (Woman clasping middle finger of Man's R hand with her L hand), who spins in place with treading steps for three revolutions clockwise		3
Partners face in a single circle (Man facing counterclockwise, Woman clockwise) as		
Man jumps to a stance with feet apart, knees slightly bent, clapping both hands to thighs, Woman stops spinning to face him, finishing with feet together, hands on hips	1	
Hold	2	

I

A. Standing in place, dancers

Clap partner's hands (R to L and L to R) in front at shoulder level	3	4
Clap own hands behind back, arms straight	1	
Clap own hands in front of chest	2	5
Clap partner's hands in front at shoulder level	3	6
Repeat claps as analyzed in Meas. 5		

B. *Woman*, hands on hips, spins continuously clockwise with treading steps, progressing slightly in a counterclockwise direction, gauging turns to face Man on Ct. 1 of Meas. 12.

while

Man follows with [See Plate 7]

(1) Leap to R foot, at same time slapping sole of L foot in back with R hand (L knee is bent so that L leg crosses in back of R knee)	1	
Slap front of L thigh with L hand, L knee raised forward	&	
Slap front of R thigh with R hand	2	
Slap front of L thigh with L hand	&	
Slap sole of L foot, crossed in back of R knee, with R hand (as in Ct. 1)	3	7
(2) Step L	1	
Slap front of L thigh with L hand, at same time bringing R leg up in front, knee bent, to	2	8
Slap inside of R ankle with R hand	3	
Repeat B		9-10
Repeat (1) of B as analyzed for Meas. 7		11

Plate 7

Schuhplattler

71

	COUNTS	MEASURES

Partners facing in a single circle,
    Man steps L in place to face Woman who stops spinning to face
    him 1
    Hold 2
    Clap partner's hands in front at shoulder level 3   12
Repeat A and B three times, beginning each repetition with Ct. 1 of
Meas. 5. On last measure of third repetition (Meas. 20, 2nd ending)
    Woman continues spinning

while

Man dances
    Step L 1
    Hold 2
    Step R 3   13-20
                               5-20
                               2nd
                             ending

II

A. Couples move counterclockwise around the circle.
    Woman continues spinning clockwise as in Figure I

while

Man follows her bending slightly forward with
    Leap lightly L, R foot lifted off the floor in back, R knee bent
    sharply 1
    Clap palm of R hand against a circle formed by the joining of the
    thumb and index finger of the L hand (cupped in a loose fist) to
    make a hollow sound 2
    Hold 3   21
    Repeat 7 times, leaping alternately to R, L, R, L, etc. Intermit-
    tently, the Man may flip the hem of the Woman's skirt with R
    hand as if to give her added momentum in the spin . . .   22-28
B. In closed social dance position (Man beginning L, Woman R),
    couples turn clockwise while progressing counterclockwise around
    the circle with
    7 waltz steps   21-27
    During the seventh waltz step, the Woman places her L hand be-
    hind her back, palm out, Man reaches under Woman's L arm to
    grasp Woman's L hand with his R hand. Man turns Woman R in
    place under her R arm 1
    Man drops to R knee for finish—partners facing opposite direc-
    tions, leaning back and looking at each other, Man kneeling on
    R knee, Woman's R hand clasped in Man's L behind his neck,
    Woman's L hand clasped in Man's R behind her back. [See
    Bavarian couple on Swiss and German Costume Plate] . . 2
    Hold position 3   28

SCHUHPLATTLER—A COUPLE DANCE

Bavaria

SCHUHPLATTLER — A DANCE FOR TWO MEN

The origin and significance of the *Schuhplattler* — *A Dance for Two Men* — is given in the introductory material which precedes the description of the *Schuhplattler* as a couple dance. The *Schuhplattler* for two men is a dance imitative of the fighting of two large male black grouse or falcons native to Bavaria. The various movements suggestive of a fight are executed dramatically with vigorous participation on the part of both dancers. The style for the performance of the dance is the same as described for the man's clapping part in the introduction to the *Schuhplattler* for a man and a woman.

This ancient dance for two men is an exciting drama in rondo form, the challenge figure recurring throughout with increasingly ferocious movements, interspersed with hoarse cries and shrill whistles in imitation of the sounds made by the male birds from which the dance stems. Each alternate figure introduces a new rhythmic pattern achieved through the accents resulting from various stamping, clapping, and beating movements. The final challenge figure terminates the dance with victory for one dancer and defeat for the other.

This *Schuhplattler* is very similar in idea and type of movements included — ear-boxing, fist-shaking, hair-pulling, *et cetera* — to the *Oxen Dance* of Sweden, a dance for two men included in *Folk Dances of Scandinavia*.[1] A traditional type of dance for two men, this *Schuhplattler* is particularly suitable for boys and men.

Formation: Any number of couples (comprised of two Men) arranged informally about the room, each Man on either side of a specific dancing area allocated to him and his partner.

Introduction

	COUNTS	MEASURES
Two Men enter from either side of their specific dancing area to positions eight or ten feet apart, facing each other, with		
6 running steps (beginning R)	1&,2&, 3&	6
Dancers face each other and dance		
Stamp R foot vigorously, slapping R thigh with R hand	1	
Slap L thigh raised slightly in front with L hand	2	
Still facing, with bent arms extended to the side and diagonally upward, palms of hands forward, fingers straight and spread apart		
Kick straightened L leg forward	ah	
Kick straightened R leg forward, bringing L leg down from kick to receive weight (scissors kick)	3	7
Stamp R vigorously	1	
Hold, glaring at each other, transferring weight to L	2,3	8

I
Challenge

Dancers move clockwise in a small circle, facing throughout, with the following pulsing step which should suggest a stealthy walk:

Step R with bent knee, ankle, and hip 1

---

[1]Duggan, *et al, op. cit.*

	COUNTS	MEASURES

Rise slowly to ball of R foot, R knee straight, raising L leg in front with L knee bent 2,3   1

Repeat 6 times alternating L, R, L, R, etc.   2-7

During this stealthy circling, *Man 1* bends his arms (Ct. 1) and straightens them out to the side and diagonally upward, palms of hands forward, fingers straight and spread apart (Cts. 2,3), rising as high as he can as though attacking *Man 2*

while

Man 2 crouches low, elbows bent with hands close to shoulders, palms forward, fingers spread, as if to avoid an attack from Man 1. [See Plate 8, page 76]

On Meas. 2, *Man 1* crouches while *Man 2* bends and straightens arms, rising as tall as possible. Continue alternating the two movements. Intermittently, one dancer may utter a hoarse cry which is answered by the other man.

Still facing, dancers jump to a stance with feet apart, knees bent, at the same time uttering a cry or war whoop and running fingers through hair as if to prepare for a fight 1

Hold 2,3   8

II

Shoe-Clapping

A. Still facing each other, both dancers

Stamp R vigorously, without weight. 1

Slap R thigh raised in front (R knee bent) with R hand 2

Slap sole of R foot with L hand (the R foot is brought inward toward the left from the bent knee position of Ct. 2) 3   1

Leap R and at the same time slap the sole of the L foot (raised in back of R knee, L knee bent) with the R hand 1

Kick straightened L leg forward . . . . ah

Kick straightened R leg forward and touch R toe with R hand, bringing L leg down from kick to receive weight (scissors kick) . 2

Bend R leg at knee, R thigh still lifted, and slap R thigh with R hand 3   2

B. To assume a crouched stride stance, both dancers

Bring the R foot down to step about 12 inches from and to the R side of the L foot, slapping R thigh with R hand 1

Slap L thigh with L hand . . . . &

Slap R thigh with R hand 2

Slap L thigh with L hand . . . . &

Bringing L foot (L knee bent) up in front of R thigh, slap sole of L foot with R hand 3

Slap L thigh with L hand; L foot remaining in lifted position . &   3

Return to stance,

Plate 8

Schuhplattler

	COUNTS	MEASURES
Stepping L about 12 inches from and to the L side of the R foot, slapping R thigh with R hand	1	
Slap L thigh with L hand	&	
Slap R thigh with R hand	2	
Slap L thigh with L hand	&	
Bringing R foot (R knee bent) up in front of L thigh, slap sole of R foot with L hand	3	
Slap R thigh with R hand; R foot remaining in lifted position .	&	4

NOTE: Throughout this part, the knees are bent and relaxed with stance kept alive by keeping both feet on the floor, with weight on balls of feet and shifting weight from side to side during the clapping and slapping.

Repeat A and B except for Ct. 3& of B, instead of which dancers

	COUNTS	MEASURES
Jump forward to both feet to positions in the crouched stance about five feet from each other with feet apart and strike both thighs with the hands (L hand on L thigh, R on R)	3	
Hold	&	5-8

III

Challenge With Shoulder Pushing

	MEASURES
With fists clenched in front of body at waist level, elbows to side, dancers use the same stealthy, pulsing step as analyzed in Figure I, to challenge further by alternately stepping R toward each other, pushing R shoulder against R shoulder (Meas. 9) and stepping L apart (Meas. 10) as they circle clockwise about each other	9-15
Jump apart and hold as at finish of Figure I	16

IV

Fist Beating

A. Facing each other, dancers

	COUNTS	MEASURES
Stamp R, dropping L knee to the floor in a crouched kneel (ball of L foot remains on floor), beating knuckles of R fist against floor in front of R foot	1	
Beat knuckles of L fist against floor beside R fist	&	
Repeat alternately beating R and L knuckles against floor 10 times to make 12 times in all	2&,3&, 1&,2&, 3&, etc.	9-10

B.

	MEASURES
Rock back on ball of L foot to standing position and dance Meas. 3-4 as described in B of Figure II	11-12
Repeat A	13-14
Repeat Meas. 7-8 as described in B of Figure II jumping to position about four feet apart	15-16

V

Challenge With Hair Pulling

COUNTS   MEASURES

With arms to side, elbows bent, palms of hands to front, fingers spread, dancers use the same stealthy, pulsing step as analyzed for Figure I, circling clockwise about each other, to challenge again by alternately stepping R toward each other, Man 1 grabbing hair of Man 2 with R hand (Meas. 17) and stepping L apart (Meas. 18), releasing grasp on hair. Man 1 snatches at the hair of Man 2 on Meas. 17 & 21, Man 2 snatching hair of Man 1 on Meas. 19 & 23   17-23

    Jump to positions about three feet apart and hold stance as at finish of Figure I   24

VI

Hand-Clapping

A. Facing each other, dancers
    Stamp R foot vigorously in place, taking weight   1
    Lift L leg forward with knee bent, clap own hands under L knee, weight R, body remaining erect   2
    Clap own hands in front of chest, weight on both feet . . .   3   17
    Clap own R hand against partner's R hand   1
    Clap own L hand against partner's L hand   2
    Clap own hands   3   18
B. Repeat Meas. 3-4 as described in B of Figure II   19-20
    Repeat A   21-22
    Repeat Meas. 7-8 as described in B of Figure II   23-24

VII

Challenge With Fist-Shaking

With the same stealthy pulsing step as analyzed in Figure I, dancers now challenge by alternately stepping R toward each other shaking R fists vigorously in opponent's face (Meas. 17) and stepping L apart (Meas. 18) as they circle clockwise about each other, gradually widening circle   25-31

    Jump to a distance about twelve feet apart and hold as at finish of Figure I   32

VIII

Ear-Boxing

A. Turning R shoulders toward each other, weight on L feet, dancers
    Hop L traveling sideward toward each other, R leg extended to the side   1
    Step R forward toward each other   2
    Step L forward toward each other   3   25

	COUNTS	MEASURES

B. Imitating boxing of ears,
   Man 1 swings R hand as if to box the L ear of Man 2, Man 2 claps
   own hands in front to make the sound of a slap 1
   Repeat, Man 2 swinging and Man 1 clapping 2
   Man 1 swings again, Man 2 ducking to R and clapping . . . 3   26

C. Dancers move apart as though staggering back from blows with
   3 hops backward on the L foot, R leg lifted with bent knee . . 1,2,3   27

D. Repeat Meas. 3 as described in B of Figure II   28
   Repeat A, B, C and D   29-32

IX

Challenge with Victory and Defeat

Repeat Meas. 1-6 as described in Figure I   33-38
   Man 1 raises his R arm and swings it down toward Man 2 who
   falls to the ground as if in defeat   39
   Man 1 throws his hands up and shouts a cry of victory (he may
   place his foot on the body of Man 2 in further boast of his triumph)   40

SCHUHPLATTLER—A DANCE FOR TWO MEN   *Bavaria*

FOLK DANCES OF RUSSIA AND CENTRAL EUROPE

Russia and Central Europe

GEOGRAPHICAL BACKGROUND

Russia — The Union of Soviet Socialist Republics represents the largest country in the world. The extent of its territory, a total of 8,433,000 square miles, covers one-sixth of the land surface of the world and is approximately equal to that of the entire continent of North America. The U.S.S.R. is bounded on the west by Rumania, Hungary, Poland, the Baltic Sea, and Finland; on the north by the Arctic Ocean; on the east by the Pacific Ocean; and on the south by the Black and Caspian Seas and the Asiatic countries of Turkey, Iran, Afghanistan, China, Mongolia, and Manchuria. Geographically, the country may be divided into European Russia and Asiatic Russia. The European Russian terrain consists of plains which slope gradually to the seas surrounding the country with the highest sections in the hilly areas about Moscow and Leningrad. The Ural Mountains separate European Russia from Asiatic Russia. The rich plains and forest areas of the steppes lie on the far side of the mountainous regions. The farthermost north or tundra region remains frozen during the greater portion of each year; the meager grasses which grow there, however, may be used for pasturage during the summer months. The chief rivers of Russia are the Volga, the largest river on the European continent, and the Dnieper. The colorful and historic Volga is navigable for almost all of its 2,200 miles of length and flows south into the Caspian Sea. The Dnieper River in Western Russia flows into the Black Sea.

Russia is a country with fabulous resources including rich deposits of all types of minerals and metals and vast areas of timber land. Until the Revolution, farmers worked the land with hand tools and managed, by dint of long hours of labor, to raise only enough food for their families. Now that machinery and cooperative enterprise have been initiated into Russia, those that work on the land are able to produce food in much larger quantities than previously. Russia ranks first in the production of wheat among the nations of Europe. At present only about one-eighth of Russia's vast expanse of land is under cultivation.

The growing manufacturing industry of Russia produces cotton and woolen fabrics, woodwork articles, motor tires, good leather articles, and rivals the French in the making of fine soaps, perfumes and eau de colognes.

Czechoslovakia — The Republic of Czechoslovakia is a narrow strip of land in Central Europe constituting an area of 49,373 square miles, slightly larger than that of the state of Louisiana. Czechoslovakia is bounded on the south by Austria and Hungary, on the west and north by Germany, on the north by Poland, and on the east by Russia.

The Carpathian Mountains range along the Polish border in the northern section of the country. From these mountains, the land slopes down to the south and into the Hungarian plains. The western section of Czechoslovakia forms two large lowland basins surrounded by mountains which rise into the Sudeten ranges in the western and southwestern parts of the country. The Danube River separates Czechoslovakia from Hungary for a part of its course through Southern Europe.

The climate on the plains and in the mountains of Czechoslovakia is typical of that of Continental Europe — hot during the summer and very cold during the winter except in the western lowlands area where it is milder throughout the year. Rainfall is heaviest in the mountainous region but adequate throughout the country.

The fertile, arable lands of Czechoslovakia provide occupation for about one-third of the population in the cultivation of cereals — especially oats, barley, rye, wheat, and corn — sugar beets, potatoes, hops, and fruit orchards. Cattle, pigs, sheep, goats, and horses are raised in abundance. The republic is fortunate in its extensive and fine forests of maple, ash, oak, walnut, and cherry trees which cover approximately one-third of the surface of the land.

Mineral deposits are rich, especially in coal, iron, petroleum, antimony, graphite, gold, silver, copper, lead, and rock salts.

Manufacturing in Czechoslovakia is centered about textile mills — in which cotton, linen, and woolen fabrics are woven — glass works, paper mills, furniture factories, and the making of numerous small manufactured articles including those carved from wood.

Hungary — The Republic of Hungary, situated in Southern Europe, comprises an area of 61,891 square miles, slightly larger than that of Georgia, one of the United States of America. Hungary is bounded on the south by Yugoslavia, on the east by Rumania and Russia, on the north by Czechoslovakia, and on the west by Austria.

The topography of Hungary represents a great plains region which sweeps down from the highlands of Austria on the west to the valleys surrounding the Danube River and the Tisza, its tributary, and upward to the Carpathian Mountains in the eastern and northeastern sections of the country. The climate in Hungary is typical of that of Central Europe with mild, sometimes hot, summers and bitterly cold winters. The annual precipitation provides enough moisture for agricultural needs with the greater portion of the rainfall occurring during the summer months.

Hungary is primarily an agricultural country; its chief crops are wheat and other grain cereals, potatoes, sugar beets and important vineyards, especially around Tokay in Northeast Hungary. The excellent, natural grasslands of the Hungarian plains have given rise to an extensive ranching industry. Some of the finest horses, cattle, and sheep of Europe are bred on these plains. Hungary has one of the largest bauxite deposits in the world.

Yugoslavia — The Republic of Yugoslavia constitutes an area of 96,000 square miles, slightly smaller than the state of Oregon. Yugoslavia is bounded on the southwest by the Adriatic Sea, on the south by Greece and Albania, on the east by Bulgaria and Rumania, on the north by Austria and Hungary, and on the west by Italy. The topography of the country is primarily mountainous in nature. A portion of the Alpine system of Europe, the Julian and Dinaric Alps, ranges along the Adriatic coast. The eastern section of the country is covered by a part of the Carpathian system of mountains. Between these eastern and western mountainous sections are the rich plains, river valleys, and uplands regions which extend diagonally across the country. The Danube and the Tisza Rivers flow through Yugoslavia, as well as a number of lesser rivers. There are beautiful lakes, mineral springs, and resort areas in the mountains and along the coast which attract a sizeable tourist trade during various seasons of the year. The climate of Yugoslavia is typical of that prevalent on the continent of Europe; the winters are cold and the summers, especially in the plains regions, are hot.

The leading industry of this country is agriculture which is carried on by individual farmers with relatively small sections of land. The chief crops, raised primarily in the plains areas, are cereals—wheat, oats, barley, and corn—vegetables, orchards of the various fruits which thrive in a temperate climate, grapevines, sugar beets, flax, and tobacco. Pigs are raised in larger numbers than any other livestock although many cattle, horses, and sheep are bred also. The leading mineral deposits in Yugoslavia include coal, iron, copper, gold, and lead. The industries ranking next to that of agriculture in importance are flour milling, lumbering, weaving, brewing and distilling, and fishing in the Adriatic Sea.

HISTORICAL AND SOCIOLOGICAL BACKGROUND

Russia—The earliest known inhabitants of Russia were the Slavic and Finno-Ugrian tribes of people who inhabited a forest region of Northern Russia along the Dnieper River. Early in the ninth century, Vikings from Scandinavia spread across the North Sea, some traveling on into England and some crossing the Baltic to sail up the rivers of Russia. One of these Norsemen, Rurik, organized the various Slavic tribes around Novgorod and established in 862 a kingdom under his reign in this section of the country. The Finns called these Vikings *Róus* and later Arabic historians, in accounts of their invasions of the Caspian and Black Seas, called them Russians. Rurik's successors—Oleg, who reigned from 879 to 912, and Igor, who reigned from 912 to 945—enlarged Rurik's original kingdom by further conquests. Under Vladimir "the Great," in 988, the Russians were converted to Greek Orthodoxy. During the thirteenth and fourteenth centuries, hordes of Tartars from the northeast invaded the country; descendants of these Tartan tribes comprise a large element in the population of the U.S.S.R. today.

During the thirteenth century, the Mongols, under Ghenghis Khán, overran Northern Asia, checking the brief beginnings of Eastern Civilization in Russia and making vassals of the Christian princes reigning there. It was not until the fifteenth century that Ivan III, or Ivan "the Great," (1462-1505) of Moscow overthrew the Mongol rule, conquered the republic of Novgorod, and began the development of the present Russian Empire. The influence of Constantinople on Russian art and religion was greatly strengthened during the reign of this sovereign, an influence which continues to be strong. In 1547, Ivan IV, or Ivan "the Terrible," was the first Russian ruler to assume the title of czar.

In 1613, Michaél Feódorovich was elected czar of Russia by an assembly of noblemen and was the first ruler of the famous Romanov line. In reality, Russia's progress as a western power began with the reign of Peter "the Great," the "Father of Modern Russia," in 1689. Peter introduced many of the progressive ideas of the more advanced nations of Western Europe although his policies were strenuously opposed by the nobility. After his death, much of the development which he had sponsored lapsed until the reign of Catharine II (1762-1796), when progress in Russian civilization was accelerated again and this country was recognized by other nations as a great world power. During the reign of Catharine, a section of Poland was acquired, adding 180,000 square miles of territory and 6,000,000 inhabitants to Russia and, through successful warfare, the Crimea and other territories which comprise the Ukraine were wrested from the Turks.

Under Alexander I (1801-1825), Russia's relations with Napoleon were alternately friendly and hostile and at times severed altogether. Napoleon marched his army across Russia to the gates of Moscow which the Russians surrendered to him. While he waited for a peace proposal, the Russians burned Moscow and forced a retreat of the French army. As winter was coming on and Napoleon's men were in a weakened condition, the Russian army was successful in driving them back across Russia, thus bringing to an end Napoleon's ambitious campaign. Alexander I began the abolition of serfdom in the Baltic provinces, a reform which Alexander II extended throughout the Empire, thus freeing more than 20,000,000 men in 1861. In spite of an increase in reforms enacted to aid the masses of the people in Russia, there prevailed a growing spirit of revolution during the regime of Alexander II and, in 1881, he was assassinated by revolutionary conspirators in St. Petersburg, which is now called Leningrad. Alexander III, who succeeded Alexander II to the throne, extended the Russian dominion into Asia and began the famous Trans-Siberian Railway system. He also initiated a cruel persecution of the Jews in Russia which finally incited protests from other nations. Nicholas II, who replaced his father as ruler in 1894, brought about the completion of the Trans-Siberian Railway and constructed other important transportation lines in Asia. A treaty with China gave Russia the right to build the Manchurian Railway and, on the pretext of guarding this railway, Russia occupied Manchuria with troops and thereby provoked a declaration of war from Japan some eight years later. After a short conflict, Russia accepted the Treaty of Portsmouth under which she withdrew from both Manchuria and Korea.

Of even greater significance than the defeat of Russia by Japan, however, were the social and political movements within the Empire itself which were a direct outgrowth of the Russo-Japanese War. The thinking people of all classes realized that Russia's defeat in this war was facilitated by the corrupt and inefficient bureaucracy which the czar either could not or would not control. In addition to this factor, the government offered no relief from the land system which permitted people of certain sections to starve while Russian crops were exported to feed other nations. A rapidly growing labor class, centered in the cities, began a rumbling of protest which was to culminate in a revolution.

In 1905, a revolution flared throughout Russia in the form of strikes. An attempt on the part of the government to break one of the strikes in St. Petersburg resulted in the death of over five hundred innocent persons by the police and soldiers of the czar. Finally, however, the ruling power realized that such repressive measures would not ameliorate the situation and a constitution was drafted which provided for the election by the people of a national assembly as a part of the government of the country. This assembly, the Duma, proved of little value since the czar reserved the right to dissolve it whenever he saw fit. When the first Duma attempted to inaugurate legislation to better conditions of the people through a universal right of franchise, reform in the land laws to remedy the national food crisis, and the abolition of the council of the Empire, the czar at once dissolved the Duma in 1906.

The fundamental causes of the Russian Revolution of 1917 lay in the political and economic structure of Russia. The czar and his bureaucratic government, the nobility, the clergy, and the wealthy bourgeois had control of the government, land, and general wealth. These groups represented a very small minority of the people. The masses of Russians were the land-poor peasants and the underprivileged, exploited industrial workers. Conflict between the government and the people had almost reached a breaking point when Russia entered World War I, thus uniting the people of that nation in a common cause. As the war progressed, the bungling of the bureaucratic government became a threat to the nation in that vital materials could not be sent to the front as rapidly as they were needed.

The Zemstvos Union was formed with Prince Lvóv at its head; its purpose was to work for the advancement of the army which it accomplished with such growing success that Russian forces made encouraging gains in the spring of 1916. With the appointment of a German sympathizer as Foreign Minister in the Russian government, however, matters became steadily worse and resulted, finally, in the abdication of Nicholas II and the collapse of the government in March of 1917. The Ministry connected with the old regime was overthrown, some of its personnel imprisoned, and the government of Russia came under the control of the Duma and a new Ministry led by liberals. The task of forming a stable government was difficult, especially in a nation at war. The situation was further complicated by Nikolai Lenin, a radical leader, and his followers who united with the radical group in the peasants' revolutionary party to form the Bolshevik party. This group advocated an immediate separate peace with Germany and attempted to overthrow the new government. Alexander Kerensky, who became Premier on July 22, 1917, struggled for a brief time against disorganization promoted by Lenin and his followers but, on November 7, 1917, lost control of the government to Lenin. This placed Russia under the control of two outstanding Bolsheviks — Lenin and Trotsky. In the spring of 1918, Lenin accepted the German terms in the Treaty of Brest-Litovsk for a separate peace with Germany which was signed on March 3, 1918. The period which followed was one of revolution in the truest sense of the word. Every aspect of Russian life was affected. Private lands were made public, natural resources were placed under governmental control, and the laborers were placed in charge of the factories. Nicholas II and his family were murdered in their Siberian prison.

Civil war soon prevailed in many sections of Russia but was curbed by Trotsky's well-organized Red army. Finally, by 1920, the entire nation was under the control of the Soviet government although the years of 1919 and 1920 were exceedingly difficult ones for the new regime due to the internal disruption and the generally demoralized morale of the people. In 1921, great sections of Russia were swept with famine and disease which brought about the death of thousands of persons. In this same year, however, the New Economic Policy was inaugurated, restoring to capitalists the control of small factories and to the peasants the control of the farms. In 1923, a constitution for the Union of the Soviet Socialist Republics was drawn up and adopted by the first All-Union Congress.

Nikolai Lenin died in 1924. In the ensuing struggle for control between Stalin and Trotsky, Stalin was victor and assumed an important role in the Soviet government in 1926.

Two years later the widely-known Five Year Plan for National Economic Construction was put into effect and resulted in greatly increased production in all industries. In 1933 the second Five Year Plan was begun with emphasis placed primarily upon the light industries including the production of textiles, clothing, and other articles of immediate use to the people of Russia.

In 1934 Joseph Stalin, who was secretary-general of the Communist Party, became a member of the Presidium, a committee responsible for governing the Soviet Union between sessions of the Union Congress. In 1936, the U.S.S.R. adopted a democratically worded Constitution. Political power continued to be vested in the Communist Party. In 1937 began the purges to eradicate as many of the original Bolsheviks, who now opposed Stalin's policies, as possible. Questionable secret trials were held and wholesale executions of the early leaders of the Communist Party took place. In preparation for his Polish war of aggression in Europe in 1939, Hitler signed a non-aggression pact with Stalin. Two days after the collapse of Poland, Russia and Germany divided their spoils. To strengthen her defense, Russia began making demands of her own for territory, including a portion of Finland, the Baltic republics of Estonia, Latvia, Lithuania, and a section of Rumania. Russia's foreign policy with Germany came to an abrupt about-face in 1941 when Hitler attacked the Soviet Union on all fronts. Russia then joined the Allied Nations against Germany in World War II and contributed to the unconditional surrender of the Axis Powers in 1945.

The people of Russia are divided geographically and politically into sixteen soviet socialist republics. These republics are: the Russian Socialist Federated Soviet Republic which includes most of European Russia and all of Siberia; the seven republics which border on the rest of Europe—Karelia, Estonia, Latvia, Lithuania, White Russia, the Ukraine and Moldavia; the three republics of the Caucasus region—Georgia, Armenia, and Azerbaijan; and the five republics in Central Asia—Turkoman, Uzbek, Tadjik, Kirghiz, and Kazak.

The people of the U.S.S.R. may be divided roughly into five groups. The majority of the Russians—153,000,000 in number, which is approximately three-fourths of the total population of this nation—are of Slavic heritage and include the "Great Russians" who have Moscow as their central city and the Ukrainians, or "Little Russians," and the White Russians who are centered about the city of Kiev. These Slavic groups adhere primarily to the Greek Orthodox Faith. The group next in size is the Turco-Tartars who number approximately 21,000,000 and live in the areas of Crimea, Kazan, Azerbaijan, Uzbek, and Kazak. The people in these republics are characterized by their dark skins and slanting eyes. They are predominantly Mohammedan in religion. The Japhetic people number about 7,000,000 and follow a variety of religious beliefs. They include the Armenians, the Cherkessians, the Khevsurs, and the Georgians. These people have olive skins. Stalin, a Georgian, is probably the most distinguished native son of that particular republic. The Finno-Ugrians, approximately 5,000,000 in number, live in the republics of Estonia and Karelia. There are approximately 2,000,000 Jews in the U.S.S.R. (1947).

Throughout Russia's history, and especially during the reigns of the last czars, there was continuous conflict between the mixed racial groups of the country. The animosities were the result of the exploitation and oppression of the weaker peoples by three powerful ruling groups of Russia—the nobility, the military, and the clergy. This history of oppression is credited by some as the cause of the melancholy quality and minor mode of many Russian folk songs. The 1936 Constitution of Russia declared hatred or persecution of any minority groups in that country a crime against the Russian state and one punishable by law. This specific article of legislation states that all citizens, regardless of their race, or of their social, political, and economic status, are entitled to equal rights.

From the start the Communists have been largely anti-church because of the close tie-up between the Greek Orthodox Church and the czarist regimes. The Bolsheviks who ruled Russia following World War I looked upon religion as a force sponsored by capitalistic interests as a palliative for the oppressed and regarded it as one of the causes of their long period of subjugation. They attempted, therefore, to destroy the church in Russia by nationalizing church property and bringing to trial church dignitaries. The harsh sentences passed upon these men of the church brought cries of indignation from Western Europe and caused the government of Russia to retreat in its campaign against them. A second attempt to sponsor the proposed spread of atheism was made through propaganda but it, also, proved unsuccessful. In 1929, a third attempt, directed by the Union of the Godless—an organization sponsored by the Russian state—barred the church from any activity other than that of conducting religious services, and instigated anti-religious teaching in the schools and among adult groups throughout the country. This program also failed and, in 1943, the Russian government authorized the restoration of the patriarchate. Colleges for training priests were established, priests were again granted the right of franchise, feasts on the church calendar again became rest days, and the observation of Sunday as the Sabbath in its original sense was restored.

Russia is a land with great potential wealth. The social and industrial revolutions in this country took place later than those in most of the other nations of Europe so that Russia actually has not begun to measure the extent of her resources. Because of the tremendous size of the country and the masses of her peoples, the task of utilizing the raw materials of Russia so that they serve the people and contribute to the advancement of a nation in which the standard of living is optimum and in which everyone has an adequate livelihood is a gigantic one. The Communist Party has chosen to accomplish this task through a highly organized and closely supervised system of control of the nation's key positions of authority in industry and in government by highly trained party members. The objectives of the party and the procedures for reaching these ends are not always understandable to those who live outside of Russia. The success of the party in the solution of Russia's internal problems as well as in the role which they choose for her to assume in international affairs awaits the perspective of future time. Russia has enriched culture by the contributions of Tolstoy, Chekhov, and Dostoyevsky in literature; and of Tschaikowsky, Rachmaninoff, Shostakovitch, Rimsky-Korsakoff, and Stravinsky in music. Modern psychology, for a time, drew much from the work of Ivan Pavlov.

Czechoslovakia—As early as the sixth century, the Slavic people known as Czechs were settled in Bohemia. The Czechs, always maintaining a vital spirit of nationality, developed Bohemia into a strong European power. Bohemia was able to resist Germanization of the kingdom until 1526 when the Habsburg family came into power and Bohemia was subjugated to Austrian rule. As a result of many wars fought in Bohemia — attributable, in part, to her location between Austria, Hungary, and Germany — the Czechs lost a large portion of their political independence.

With the beginning of World War I, the sympathy of the Czechs lay chiefly with the Allies but their geographic position made anything but assistance to the Germanic powers impossible. All Czechs of military age were conscripted and placed in the Austro-Hungarian army. During the course of the war, thousands of the Czechs deserted or surrendered in large groups to the Allies. In 1917, after the beginning of Czechoslovakian organization in Paris by Thomas G. Masaryk and Eduard Benes, an independent Czechoslovakian army was established in France. This newly-formed organization was known as the National Czechoslovak Council.

At the close of World War I, the Republic of Czechoslovakia was created by combining the adjacent states of Bohemia, Moravia and Silesia, Slovakia, and Carpathian Ruthenia. The country was occupied by the Nazis in 1939. With the defeat of Germany in 1945, Czechoslovakia was restored to her pre-war status with the exception of Ruthenia which was ceded to the Soviet Union. Shortly after the beginning of 1948 the influence of Communism, which had begun to pervade the country, was instrumental in the formation of a Communist Government and the dissolution of opposing parties.

The present population of Czechoslovakia is estimated at 14,000,000 people of whom only about two-thirds are Czechs or Slovaks; the minority group is composed of Germans, Magyars, Ruthenians, Jews, and Poles. The predominant religion is the Roman Catholic Faith. Czechoslovakia's famous men include John Huss, the religious reformer, John Amos Comenius, one of the founders of modern education, Karol Capek, novelist and playwright, and Friedrich Smetana and Antonin Dvorak, composers.

Hungary — The Hungarians, who are correctly referred to as Magyars, entered the present territory of Hungary during the beginning of the tenth century. Because of their name, however, these Hungarian people should not be confused with the Huns who terrorized Europe and crushed the ancient Roman Empire. In a state of barbarism, the Hungarians conquered the Slavic tribes and made numerous settlements near the basin of the Middle Danube on the great plain southwest of the Carpathian Mountains. Before the end of the century, the Hungarians had adopted a civilized form of life, had accepted Christianity, and were rapidly assimilating Western culture.

The Hungarians were attacked and defeated by the Turks in 1526; as a result, most of the country which they had settled fell into foreign hands. In an effort to regain her former status, the Hungarian Parliament recognized the claims of the Habsburgs, sovereign family of Austria, as rulers of their lands. Finally, in 1867, Hungary regained her constitutional liberty and independence and, in the same year, the dual monarchy of Austria-Hungary was created with Emperor Francis Joseph of Austria as its ruler.

On June 24, 1914, the assassination of Archduke Francis Ferdinand, heir to the throne of Austria-Hungary, by a Serbian student precipitated World War I. At the close of the war, the dual monarchy was dissolved. Some of the lands held by the two countries were given to other nations as war gains and some sections were absorbed in the formation of new republics. Hungary, therefore, became a much smaller nation than it was prior to the war.

In World War II, Hungary fought on the side of the Nazis of Germany. Early in 1945, however, she negotiated with the Allies for a separate peace and surrendered unconditionally on January 20, 1945. By the end of that year, Hungary had elected a new parliament and was recognized once more as an independent nation.

The population of Hungary, which totals approximately 9,106,252 people, is composed largely of Magyars. The Magyars are of Finno-Ugrian stock, coming originally from Asia, and are, therefore, of the Mongolian family of races. Approximately two-thirds of the people of Hungary are members of the Roman Catholic Church; the rest, with the exception of a few Jews, adhere to some Protestant faith.

The plains of Hungary are picturesquely dotted with small houses built of sun-dried bricks in some sections of the country and of wood or stone in others. They are white-washed and appear as glistening accents against the flat landscape. Within the homes, the pride of every housewife is the bed with feather pillows fluffed full of air; the beds are embossed with beautifully embroidered sheets and pillow cases and the pillows are stacked to the ceiling in families of sufficient wealth. Additional decor within the homes manifests the skill of the Hungarians in weaving and lace-making, ceramics, wood-carving, and leather work. Hungarian cultural leaders of world fame include Ferenc Molnar, playwright, and Dohnanyi and Kodaly, composers.

Yugoslavia—When the doom of the dual-monarchy of Austria-Hungary was anticipated near the close of World War I, the Yugoslav National Council met in order to attempt a measure of organization before its inevitable collapse. Attending this Council were representatives from the former Austrian provinces of Croatia, Slovenia, Bosnia, Hercegovina, and Dalmatia. On October 9, 1918, the Council voted to join with the kingdoms of Serbia and Montenegro to form an independent state. The Council, on December 1 of that year, invited Prince Alexander, regent of Serbia, to assume regency of all of the provinces included in this new state which was called the Kingdom of the Serbs, Croats, and Slovenes. On November 20, 1921, elections to a permanent assembly were held one year before Prince Regent Alexander became King Alexander I of Yugoslavia.

On January 6, 1929, the original Constitution of 1921 was dissolved by royal proclamation, a new system of government was established, and the name of the country was changed to Yugoslavia by royal decree. This system was, in reality, a complete dictatorship with Alexander at its head. The dictatorship, however, failed to secure the cooperation of the various groups comprising Yugoslavia's total population and, in 1931, it was evident that the Croats, the Slovenes, and the Serbs actively opposed their king. On October 9, 1934, King Alexander was assassinated in France, leaving as his successor his eleven-year-old son, Peter II, as King of Yugoslavia.

When World War II began in Europe in 1939, Yugoslavia succeeded in maintaining her neutrality but was unable to escape the tension which pervaded the entire Balkan area of the continent. In March, 1941, a pact was signed with Germany making Yugoslavia an Axis partner. This resulted in an overthrow of the governing regency by young King Peter and the army who established an anti-Axis government. This new freedom did not last long, however, and by April 19, the country had been completely conquered by Germany and was occupied by Italian troops with an Italian duke as its new king. With the defeat of the Axis Powers in 1945, Yugoslavia became a republic.

The population of Yugoslavia, according to a recent census report, comprises 15,920,000 individuals. Approximately forty-nine per cent of the people are members of the Serbian Orthodox Church, thirty-seven per cent are Roman Catholics, eleven per cent are Moslems, and a very small number profess each of the Jewish, Greek Orthodox and Protestant Faiths.

The great physicists, Michael Pupin and Nikola Tesla, were of Yugoslav origin, as is Louis Adamic, the well-known American writer.

FOLK DANCES

The folk dances of the many national groups of Russia and Central Europe share similarities in terms of formations, themes, and basic steps. Certain specific characteristics of style evince the influences of one group upon another in the evolution of their respective dances.

Dances of a ceremonial nature have been handed down from former eras in the development of the cultures of these peoples. Many go back beyond the Christian era to more ancient pagan rites. Sachs speaks of whirl dances performed in Slavic countries by young girls in solicitation to their gods for rain[1] and of a dance performed on Christmas night in Silesia by men and women in which couples danced around the living fruit trees, winding a rope about each one in turn. The latter dance is similar to those of other European countries which are performed about a Maypole but harks back to still more ancient fertility dances about living trees.[2] A Ukrainian dance, *Arkon*, involves stamping movements and originally was performed as a part of spring fertility festivals. Stamping in primitive dances, according to Shambaugh, was associated with the fertility of the soil.[3] Urlin speaks of "witch dances" in Bohemia and in Hungary which were taken from the dances of the gypsies and suggests an origin of the *Hornpipe* of the British Isles in the *Barina*, a Russian gypsy dance.[4] Sachs[5] and Kirstein[6] give accounts of rather macabre death dances from the Middle Ages. At wakes in Hungary, one dancer lay on the floor with a handkerchief covering his face to represent a corpse. The men and women circled about him, uttering wailing and crying sounds, to the accompaniment of the bagpipe. Sometimes they picked him up, while he remained limp and lifeless, and danced with him. In some versions, the point in the dance at which the "corpse" was raised to join in the dance itself symbolized his resurrection. Sometimes, among the Slovakian people, the "resurrection" occurred as the dancers bent over the "corpse" and kissed him back to life.

[1]Sachs, *op. cit.*, p. 140
[2]*Ibid.*, p. 65.
[3]Mary Effie Shambaugh, *Folk Festivals* (New York: A. S. Barnes and Company, 1932), p. 94.
[4]Ethel L. Urlin, *Dancing Ancient and Modern* (New York: D. Appleton-Century Company, 1914), p. 67.
[5]Sachs, *op. sit.*, p. 106.
[6]Lincoln Kirstein, *Dance* (New York: G. P. Putnam's Sons, 1935), p. 86.

As a symbol of death and resurrection, the dance was performed at weddings in Silesia as well as in Hungary. This same theme of death and resurrection is found in a Slovakian sword dance in which the leader of the dance, depicting a vegetation spirit, "dies" and is lifted high overhead by the dancers. As they lower him, he is "resurrected" and becomes alive again.[1]

The *Makovitza* is a Russian dance of thanksgiving for the harvest in which young girls dance in a circle, eating cake made of honey and poppy-seeds.[2] *Leather Bridge* and *Bridge of Oak* are ceremonial bridge dances of Slovakian and Ukrainian origin, respectively. They stem from a belief on the part of early pagans that bridges possessed supernatural significance. Some believed bridges to be symbolic of the span between life and death; others thought them to be haunted by a jealous Land Spirit who resented the passage over the bridges by human beings from one district to another and sought vengeance, therefore, in the destruction of the bridges.[3] *Chorovod* is a ceremonial dance performed throughout Russia. One version, interspersed with the social waltzes at New Year balls in the Ukraine, is of a solemn religious nature. During the course of the dance a group may kneel and bow to the floor while using the hands and arms in a style suggestive of Oriental movement.[4]

Some of the most delightful dances from Russia and Central Europe are based upon the various occupations of the people. The movements of these dances relate to the occupations in either of two ways: they are pantomimic of the activities performed by individuals who engage in the specific occupation, or they are suggestive of the type of personality which usually characterizes the individual who follows certain specific trades. Illustrative of those in the latter category are the Ukrainian *Chumak*, a character sketch of a swaggering merchant; the Slovakian *Odzemok*, a dance about the shepherd; and the Moravian *Resnik*, a character sketch of the butcher. Illustrations of the pantomimic type of occupational dances are innumerable. *Šeucovská*, from Bohemia, is based upon the work of the cobbler; Silesia also has a cobbler's dance. *Sedloček*, from Silesia, includes the sowing and threshing movements performed by a farmer.

Russia and the countries of Central Europe have spectacular dances which enable the performer to demonstrate skill in intricate movements of the feet, in brilliant leaps or jumps, or in daring feats, as in a dance with swords. One particularly characteristic step in Slavic dances Sachs terms a "squat-fling" step in which the dancers, while in a squatting position, extend their legs alternately in a forward position. In the Ukraine, this step is termed *prisjádka*.[5] It is popularly known in the United States as the bear step. The Cossack men are particularly famous for their performance of this and other intricate steps in the *Hopák*. One version of the *Lezghínka* is a sword dance performed as a solo by men in the Ukraine in which they use three swords. Real danger exists in dancing with the swords so that performance demands courage as well as skill. *Zaporózhets*, also a sword dance from the Ukraine, involves difficult

---

[1]Sachs, *op. cit.*, p. 121.
[2]Urlin, *op. cit.*, p. 63.
[3]Shambaugh, *op. cit.*, p. 94.
[4]*Ibid.*, p. 62.
[5]Sachs, *op. cit.*, p. 30.

leaps and feats with these weapons. Sachs describes an exciting solo dance for men from the Georgias—the *Stretta*—in which the dancer "leaps back, crossing his legs in the air in so doing and whirling his body to all sides."[1]

Couple dances from Russia and Central Europe which have courtship for their theme are particularly colorful. The most characteristic feature of these dances as a whole is the change from slow to fast tempi. The two most popular courtship dances in the Caucasus are the *Lezghínka* and the *Lekuri*. These are dances of great beauty in which the man dances around the woman, sometimes dancing very close to her but never touching her—not even a portion of her clothing—and then withdrawing from her. The woman, dignified and quiet, moves with a smooth, unrestrained ease. Sometimes the man moves with an easy, gliding step and sometimes with steps which demonstrate skill and daring. The Kinneys describe a spectacular turn in one of the Hungarian couple dances, the *Szolo*, in which the woman is swung through the air from her partner's right to his left side.[2] The most popular, widely-known, and therefore national dance of Hungary is the *Csárdás* which has numerous versions. The most common version is danced in two parts—the first, slow and languid, the second, spirited and fast. Versions of the *Csárdás* are adapted also for ballroom purposes. One such version is included in the present collection of folk dances. Other couple dances with an element of courtship are the *Zalman*, or *Knight*, from Bohemia, and the *Handkerchief Dance* from Moravia. The latter appears in this collection.

Social dances performed at festivals, weddings, and other similar affairs include the Serbian *Kolo*, the Ukrainian *Katerina*, *Kolomýka*, and *Zhuraval*, or *Crane*, and the mazurka, polka, and redowa—popular ballroom forms in round dances. Couples or women dance the *Kolo* as a traditional part of wedding festivities in Serbia. During the course of the dance, individuals perform elaborate steps in the center of the circle while the other participants continue to dance as they look on.

Dances in Russia and Central European countries are performed in much the same types of design as those of other European countries. Both circular and chain formations are common throughout. One interesting variation of a dance in a circular formation is the *Mühlrad*, or Mill Wheel, performed by eight boys. Four place their feet together in the center to simulate the spokes of a wheel and are turned by the other four.[3] Young girls with garlands of flowers about their heads perform another interesting circular dance at weddings. The Russian *Pletionka*, or Braid, is illustrative of a typical chain dance.[4] The Bohemian *Motovidlo* is a type of reel in longways formation as is the *Saróca* from Moravia. *Kanafaska*, included in this book, is a delightful dance in quadrille formation.

The musical accompaniment for folk dances in this region of the world includes stringed and wind as well as percussion instruments. The violin is played in all of the countries but is especially popular in Hungary. Here, the gypsies, who wander over the plains, usually

[1]Sachs, *op. cit.*, p. 26.
[2]Margaret West and Troy Kinney, *The Dance—Its Place in Art and Life* (New York: Frederick A. Stokes Company, 1914), p. 193.
[3]Sachs, *op. cit.*, p. 272.
[4]Urlin, *op. cit.*, p. 63.

carry a violin which they play at the slightest provocation. Most historians give the gypsies credit for the preservation of the folk melodies of Hungary. They embellish or arrange these melodies according to their personal inspiration as they play. The violin, the national instrument of Hungary, has numerous legends built around it. A variation of a violin is the Russian *gudók*, a three-stringed instrument with a pear-shaped body and with a string bow like a violin. The *domra* of Russia, a guitar-like instrument, is plucked with a plectrum in the same way the guitar is played. Some authorities think the *balaláika*, a well-known triangular-shaped Russian musical instrument, is a development of the *domra*.[1]

Wind instruments are frequently used to accompany folk dance. The Hungarian *tárogató* is a flute-like instrument with a melancholy tone.[2] Russian wind instruments include the *dúdka*, a kind of vertical flute; the *zhaleika*, a double reed instrument with a single mouthpiece; and the *róg*, a sort of hunting horn. Both Russia and Hungary have an instrument similar to a bagpipe. The *volýnka*, a goatskin bag with two pipes,[3] is the Russian bagpipe and the *duda*[4] is the Hungarian. Percussion instruments include drums, the Russian *bubën*—a sort of tambourine[5]—and the *cimbalom*—a Hungarian stringed instrument played with padded hammers.[6]

FOLK COSTUMES

Throughout Russia and the Central European countries, the everyday work clothing of the peoples is quite similar with variations arising as a result of differences in climate and type of work performed. In general, however, the women of these countries wear full skirts, plain blouses with long sleeves, black stockings, sturdy shoes (boots, in some sections) and a kerchief tied around the head. Heavy woolen shawls are commonly worn by the women during cold weather. Work clothing worn by the men consists of knee-length or long, dark-colored trousers, a dark shirt, heavy shoes or boots, and hats with rather wide brims. In cold weather, the men wear coats or jackets of varying designs and colors, some of which are lined with fur to insure more warmth for outdoor work during the cold winter months.

Although the everyday attire is quite similar, the traditional folk costumes worn for festivals and special occasions differ greatly in the countries comprising this region. Variations of these traditional costumes also occur within a single country as each village has a unique dress. Some costumes, however, are more common than others and are typical of a particular country.

The folk costumes worn by the women of Russia are extremely attractive. According to Mann, all women's costumes, whether simple or elaborate in design, are beautifully embroidered.[7] The complete costume is comprised of two skirts made of thick material, one worn over the other, and a bodice, either attached to or separate from the top skirt, made of

[1]*Encyclopedia Americana* (New York: Americana Corporation, 1945 Edition), p. 293 rr.
[2]Walter Starkie, *Raggle-Taggle* (New York: E. P. Dutton and Co., Inc., 1933), p. 150.
[3]*Encyclopedia Americana*, *op. cit.*, p. 293 rr.
[4]Elizabeth C. Rearick, *Dances of the Hungarians* (New York: Bureau of Publications, Columbia University, 1939), p. 49.
[5]*Encyclopedia Americana*, *op. cit.*, p. 293 rr.
[6]Rearick, *op. cit.*, p. 49.
[7]Mann. *op. cit.*, p. 54.

embroidered linen or silk brocade. The embroidered slippers worn by many women are an interesting feature of this costume. The headdress is usually made of velvet and sometimes trimmed with pearls or other precious or simulated stones.[1]

The men's costume consists of a white linen shirt, usually brightly embroidered around the collar and cuffs; trousers made either of dark, woolen material or of the same material as the shirt; and tall leather boots or *lapots* — shoes made of plaited strips from birch or lime trees.[2] Russian men commonly wear felt hats with brims, or fur bonnets and caps.

In the southern part of Russia known as the Ukraine, the prevalent festival attire, although equally attractive, is more subdued than that worn elsewhere in Russia. The woman's costume consists of a dark skirt and bodice, a beautifully embroidered white blouse, a stiff embroidered cap, and colored boots, predominantly red, or shoes and stockings. The woman of the Ukraine frequently braids her hair with gay ribbons and flowers. These do not replace her hat, however, for she wears a stiff cap over her braids.[3]

The festival costume worn by the men of the Ukraine does not differ greatly from the one previously described for the men of Russia. They wear white linen shirts and trousers, with richly embroidered designs; colored boots, usually red; and caps of fur, wool, or straw.[4]

According to Mann, the Ukrainian men and women wear an overcoat of white, grey, or brown homespun material, trimmed with stripes or cords of varying colors.[5] In the summer, the women wear a white jacket gaily decorated with pieces of colored leather strips and various metal ornaments.[6]

Czechoslovakian costumes are very gay. The women wear white blouses with sleeves of varying designs; long, full skirts of soft material; either red or black stockings; and black leather shoes, often decorated with large silver buckles. Upon their heads, the married women wear caps decorated with colored embroidery, fancy threadwork, or lace; the unmarried girls wear a tall, crown-like headdress from the top of which hang long, varicolored ribbons which drop to the level of the waist in the back.[7] An interesting feature of the Moravian girls' costume is the collar of the blouse, similar to a sailor collar and embroidered in black or colored silk.[8]

Czechoslovakian men have handsome costumes consisting of an embroidered white shirt, a gaily decorated waistcoat of rather thick material, a knee-length coat or cape with no collar but many bright buttons, tight-fitting embroidered trousers, and top boots which come almost up to the knees. They usually wear dark felt hats with rather large brims or smaller hats without brims, decorated with flowers or feathers on either side.[9]

---

[1]Mann, *op. cit.*, p. 101.
[2]*Ibid.*, p. 101.
[3]*Ibid.*, p. 102.
[4]*Ibid.*, p. 102.
[5]*Ibid.*, p. 102.
[6]*The Folk Dancer*, June, 1945, p. 5.
[7]Mann, *op. cit.*, p. 68.
[8]*Ibid.*, p. 68.
[9]*Ibid.*, p. 69.

The costumes worn by the Hungarian women are unique and interesting. According to Rearick, the costumes, or parts of them, are pleated carefully. The women accomplish the pleating by placing large, hot loaves of bread on the material which they have folded into the correct positions.[1] Another popular feature of the Hungarian woman's costume is her stiffly starched petticoats. Sometimes as many as twelve are worn beneath the pleated skirts, giving a hoop-like effect to the skirt as a whole.[2] Some girls wear so many petticoats that they have to go out of doors to dress "since the doors of some of the houses are not large enough to allow passage when fully attired."[3]

According to some authorities the Magyars of Transylvania have the finest and most beautiful Hungarian costumes.[4] Here the women wear long, full skirts of a dark color, green and blue predominating; an apron as long as the skirt and elaborately embroidered along the bottom; a second apron short enough to allow the colored border of the first apron to be seen; and a white, long-sleeved blouse with a gay red bolero. Red boots and flowered scarves complete the costume.[5]

Rearick describes the different styles of headdress worn in Hungary and explains the significance of each type. In some villages, elaborately beaded headdresses signify that the wearer has been married less than a year. Unmarried girls wear their hair in one long braid with a colored bow tied to the end.[6]

The Magyar costume worn by the man is very distinctive. His shirt and trousers, called *gatyas*, are made of white linen. The shirt has long, wide sleeves which are beautifully embroidered around the cuffs. Some of the shirts are trimmed with lace. The embroidered trousers, with lace borders of attractive design, are so full at the bottom that they resemble a skirt. Over their trousers the men wear elaborate aprons. Their boots are partially hidden by their trousers. A high felt hat with flowers attached at the back or decorated with colored feathers completes the costume.[7]

One of the most important parts of the Hungarian man's costume is his long mantle or cape, worn traditionally by the men of the plains and considered a priceless possession. These capes are made of heavy cloth or felt, and are decorated with leather designs of various colors. Worn loosely about the shoulders, the cape hangs down to the man's knees.

The festival costumes worn by the women of Yugoslavia are similar to those worn by Czechoslovakian women, with variations appearing in certain sections of the country. The type which predominates in Dalmatia is the most picturesque. In this province the women wear woolen tunics of white or dark blue over long white skirts, bright colored aprons over the tunics, and white stockings and black shoes. For their headdress they wear tiny red caps to

---

[1]Rearick, *op. cit.*, p. 11.
[2]*Ibid.*, p. 14.
[3]Elizabeth P. Jacobi, "Hungary, A Kingdom Without a King." *The National Geographic Magazine*, June, 1932, p. 718.
[4]*Folk News*, February 15, 1938, p. 96.
[5]*Ibid.*, p. 97.
[6]Rearick, *op. cit.*, pp. 12-14.
[7]*Folk Dancer*, *op. cit.*, p. 97.

which are fastened long white lace veils. For festival occasions, the women place bright yellow marigolds on top of the caps.[1] The women of Serbia and Croatia dress in gay, bright costumes for special occasions. Here, again, elaborately embroidered blouses and aprons are prevalent.

The men of Yugoslavia dress in very much the same manner as the men of Hungary — long-sleeved white shirts, long full trousers, and vests and jackets of various designs and colors. The men usually wear boots instead of shoes. Their hats are of felt and resemble, in shape, those worn by the men of the United States. For festivals and gala occasions, the men sometimes cover the tops of their hats with flowers or place an ornament of some type at the side.

FOLK FESTIVALS

The festivals observed by the peoples of Russia and of the various Central European countries are similar with respect to origin and general means of celebration. This may be attributed, in part, to the geographical proximity of the countries of this region. The festivals vary, however, in the specific manner of observation. Some are predominately religious in nature; others are primarily seasonal in character although many have lost their original significance. A third group of festivals are primarily secular in origin and in the activities marking their commemoration.

Epiphany is observed on January 6 in Russia and in other countries of Central Europe in a number of different ways. In many parts of Czechoslovakia, young boys — dressed to resemble the traditional Three Kings — go from house to house seeking alms as they sing their songs about the Magi.[2] In the churches of Hungary, the priest performs a ceremony in which he sanctifies the water before going from house to house to bestow his blessings upon the occupants with the holy water. In some sections of Hungary, young boys, dressed as the Three Wise Men, visit various households in which they sing appropriate songs and collect coins for their efforts.[3] According to the Russian legend, the Three Wise Men, after seeing the star of Bethlehem, started to make their way toward it. In traveling, they met an old woman who was cleaning her house. She asked the Wise Men if they would wait for her to finish her work so that she might accompany them. They agreed to let her make the trip to Bethlehem if she could follow them after finishing her chores, but the old woman was never able to overtake them. She wandered about the country for years and, according to old folk tales, on *Epiphany Eve* she comes down the chimney of each home to leave gifts for the children. The gifts are symbolic of those presented to the Christ Child in keeping with the Biblical account of His birth.[4] In Russia, the old woman is known as *Báboushka*, and she performs traditionally the beneficence usually associated with Santa Claus in other countries.[5] *Epiphany* in Yugoslavia

---

[1] Edwin A. Grosvenor, "The Races of Europe." *The National Geographic Magazine*, December, 1918, p. 478.
[2] Spicer, *op. cit.*, p. 84.
[3] *Ibid.*, p. 165.
[4] Walsh, op. cit., p. 397-398.
[5] *Ibid.*, p. 378.

is celebrated with church services during which impressive rites in conjunction with the blessing of water are performed. After the services, the priest visits the homes of his parishioners and sprinkles them with the water thus sanctified.[1] It is an old Serbian belief that on midnight on *Epiphany Eve*, God will fulfill any wish made of Him.[2]

Carnival Week, the week preceding Lent both in Hungary and in some sections of Russia, is the gayest season of the year and is celebrated with entertainments, parties and balls. In parts of Hungary, a legend is told about two mythical beings, Prince Cibere and King Marrow Bone, the latter representing the various indulgences of life. On January 6, these two symbolic characters enter into a conflict with each other. This struggle, always won by King Marrow Bone, epitomizes the triumph of good food and wine for this particular period. On Shrove Tuesday, another conflict arises which is won by Prince Cibere.[3] The villagers bury King Marrow Bone just as Prince Cibere begins his reign which lasts throughout the Lenten period. Cibere is the name of the sour bran soup eaten during Lent.[4] In Russia, *Carnival Week* brings with it the performance of national plays, operas, ballets, and the dramatization of old folk tales.[5]

People celebrate *Palm Sunday* throughout Central Europe in a manner similar to that of other countries, augmented by a number of unique customs. In certain sections of Central Europe, pussywillows are blessed in the various churches on this holy day. Czechoslovakians and Yugoslavians take pussywillows to the fields to insure the grain against too much rain or hail. In some places, they are attached to the roofs of the homes as a protection against fire.[6] On *Palm Sunday*, the peasants of Hungary believe that the burning of an effigy of Prince Cibere, thought to reign throughout the forty days of Lent, will relieve their community of illness and will hurry spring along its way.[7] In Yugoslavia, *Palm Sunday* is observed with many charming customs, some of which are centered around the use of flowers. On the eve of *Palm Sunday*, young girls prepare a fragrant bath by placing flowers and blossoms in the water. The next day they bathe in this water believing that they will remain lovely through the year.[8]

Good Friday, or *Great Friday*, is observed generally throughout Russia and Central Europe with special church services and interesting and varying customs peculiar to each country. In Czechoslovakia, some believe that "Hidden treasures are revealed to those seeking them while the Passion Story is being read in church."[9] A portion of the day is devoted in most sections of Czechoslovakia to the coloring of the beautiful Easter eggs to be used on Easter Monday. The Hungarians associate cleanliness with *Good Friday*, necessitating the scrubbing and whitewashing of their homes prior to the day itself. All Easter baking and the decoration of eggs must be completed before *Good Friday*.[10] Russians celebrate the Friday preceding

---

[1] Spicer, *op. cit.*, pp. 335-336.
[2] *Ibid.*, p. 335.
[3] Rearick, *op. cit.*, p. 33.
[4] Spicer, *op. cit.*, p. 166.
[5] *Ibid.*, p. 86.
[6] *Ibid.*, p. 166.
[7] *Ibid.*, p. 167.
[8] *Ibid.*, p. 337.
[9] *Ibid.*, p. 87.
[10] *Ibid.*, pp. 167-168.

Easter in an interesting manner. On the evening of *Good Friday* a church service called the Epitaphion is held. This service is a mock funeral in memory of the sorrow and mourning resulting from the Crucifixion. Large crowds gather from all parts of the village to behold the image of Christ which is borne through the streets to the accompaniment of a funeral march played by a military band.[1] *Good Friday* in Yugoslavia means the burning of candles in the churches in memory of the death of Christ, as well as burial services in which an image of Christ is placed within a tomb.[2]

Easter is an important festival of Russia and Central Europe. On this day, begun with special services in the churches, many delightful customs are observed in each of these European countries. In Czechoslovakia, Easter Sunday itself is not as important as the Monday following *Easter;* nevertheless, the day is celebrated with feasting in the homes and with visiting among friends and neighbors during the afternoon. Entire families as well as their houses, animals, and other possessions, must be spotlessly clean for the festival of *Easter* in Hungary. The day symbolizes to the Hungarians "the birth of new hope and the beginning of new life."[3] The people celebrate this religious holiday by attending church services and by feasting in the homes. In many instances these feasts represent the first big meals served since the beginning of Lent. Spicer says, "Easter is the most joyous and impressive holiday of the Russian year."[4] Festivities in Russia on *Easter* would not be complete without the traditional feast of roast pig and various kinds of sausages. Included on the list of typical foods are *baba,* a large cake, and *koulich,* a cake upon which the letters XB are marked to represent the Russian words meaning "Christ is risen."[5] According to Walsh, colored eggs, a prominent feature of Easter in Russia, are carried about by adults and children. They click these eggs together in much the same fashion as people touch glasses when a toast is made to indicate mutual kindly feelings.[6] These same festivities are observed on *Easter* in Yugoslavia following the church services with appropriate *Easter* music. Spicer writes that the young people of Yugoslavia engage in an interesting sport in which the activity centers around cracking eggs together to see which person owns the strongest egg.[7] Both young and old of Croatia exchange gaily colored eggs on the afternoon of *Easter,* further emphasizing the significance of the ritual with a kiss. This double exchange of both eggs and kisses is called *Matkanje,* a popular custom signifying mutual affection and regard.[8]

One of the most interesting festivals in Central Europe is the *Easter Monday* celebration. For Czechoslovakian youngsters, this is the greatest holiday of the year.[9] This festival centers around a form of by-play between the young boys and girls. The boys weave willow branches into small whips, decorated with gay ribbons and flowers, and "whip" the girls of their

---

[1]Walsh, *op. cit.,* p. 479.
[2]Spicer, *op. cit.,* p. 339.
[3]Rearick, *op. cit.,* p. 36.
[4]Spicer, *op. cit.,* p. 292.
[5]*Ibid.,* p. 292.
[6]Walsh, *op. cit.,* p. 780.
[7]Spicer, *op. cit.,* p. 340.
[8]*Folk News,* April 1, 1937, p. 6.
[9]Spicer, *op. cit.,* p. 87.

villages "so they won't be lazy or have fleas."[1] The girls reciprocate by giving the boys their elaborately decorated Easter eggs. Thought to insure good luck, this custom is observed in both rural and urban communities of Czechoslovakia.[2] In Hungary on *Easter Monday*, a comparable custom is observed to which the youngsters look forward throughout the year. "On Easter Monday the young lads of the village decide that the girls have not been washed clean enough so they undertake to do the job themselves."[3] Forming a group and going from house to house, they capture the girls and, with much shouting and merrymaking, throw pails of water upon them. In the group are the musicians who play gypsy music to accompany these ablutionary festivities. The Hungarian girls appear on this morning in their oldest clothes so that the anticipated drenching will not damage their festival costumes.[4] As in Czechoslovakia, the girls then present their young boy friends with colorful Easter eggs.

Although the *Christmas Eve* festival is celebrated throughout Russia and Central Europe on the evening preceding the birthday of Christ, it is not observed with the same customs in all countries. In Czechoslovakia, when the first star is seen, the family gathers to eat a traditional supper of soup, fish, *housky*, or braided bread, and a raisin and almond cake.[5] Baked carp, served with a rich spicy sauce, is one of the most widely enjoyed items on the supper menu.[6] After dinner, the *Christmas Eve* festivities continue with merrymaking, telling of fortunes, singing, and dancing. Hungarians refer to the day before Christmas as *Adam and Eve Day*. They celebrate this day with the traditional Christmas tree followed by a large family dinner of fish and poppy-seed dumplings.[7] The distribution of presents and the singing of old carols complete the *Christmas Eve* festival in Hungary. In Russia, according to Walsh, both old and young are said to assemble in the villages preparatory to visiting the houses of the mayor and of other outstanding men in their respective communities. They sing Christmas carols as they progress from house to house and receive money from the town's dignitaries in return for their holiday calls. This part of the ceremony is called *Kolenda*, and means begging for money or presents. A masquerade, in which the adults disguise themselves as cows, pigs, goats, and other animals to depict those in the stables on the occasion of Christ's birth in the manger, precedes the bountiful feast served to all the villagers.[8] Spicer writes of the interesting customs observed in Yugoslavia on *Christmas Eve*, most of which center about the burning of the yule log, or *badnyak*, in every household. The men of each family arise early and, with a team of oxen, go into the forest to cut a yule log for their *Christmas Eve* festivities. It is considered bad luck if the tree selected, or any part of it, touches another tree as it falls to the ground. Later in the evening, this huge yule log is placed in the fireplace so that one end of it extends out into the room, and traditional rites accompany the starting of the fire. After a light supper of fish, beans, and vegetables, all retire except those whose duty it is to

---

[1]Spicer, *op. cit.*, p. 87.
[2]*Ibid.*, p. 87.
[3]Rearick, *op. cit.*, p. 36.
[4]Jacobi, *op. cit.*, p. 717.
[5]Spicer, *op. cit.*, p. 92.
[6]*Folk News*, December 1, 1936, p. 3.
[7]Spicer, *op. cit.*, p. 175.
[8]Walsh, *op. cit.*, p. 235.

keep the yule log burning all night in the belief that members of the family will be spared any bad luck which might befall them if the fire were allowed to spend itself.[1]

On *Christmas Day* in Russia and in other countries of Central Europe, entire families gather in their homes for reunions, feasting, and rejoicing. The traditional foods, prepared for the *Christmas Eve* festivals, are again enjoyed by all and, in some countries, are supplemented by even more varieties of cakes and fancy pastries. In some sections of Hungary, the pagan custom of minstrelsy is still in evidence on *Christmas Day*. According to Rearick, "the minstrels go about from house to house to cast their spells, to bring either good or evil."[2] Parties for the children, masquerade balls, and other social events make *Christmas* in Russia a very gay occasion for all.[3] In Yugoslavian communities, the early hours of *Christmas Day* find a whole pig roasting on a spit.[4] A sumptuous feast is prepared for all members of the family and their friends. Many customs are observed which, according to old superstitions, will insure a plentiful harvest and other blessings throughout the ensuing year.

Celebrations held on *New Year's Day* in Russia and in Central Europe are similar in many respects. In general, they feature fortune telling, feasting, and visiting among families and friends.

May Day, celebrated on May 1 in Czechoslovakia and Hungary, features customs associated with the traditional Maypole. On the evening preceding *May Day* Czechoslovakians erect the Maypole beside the house of the most popular girl in the village. All gather there later in the day for singing, dancing, and rejoicing over the coming of spring.[5] In some Hungarian villages, the young men place May trees beside the homes of the girls whom they have chosen to marry. In other villages, only one tree is erected for the entire village.[6]

In Central Europe, the festival known variously as *St. John's Day* and *St. John's Eve* is observed with the building of traditional bonfires around which the young people dance and sing. This festival occurs either on the evening of June 23 or of June 24. In Central Europe, people believe that herbs gathered on this day will prove to have supernatural powers of healing. Hungarians sometimes call this festival *St. Ivan's Fire.*[7]

The annual Harvest festival, known in some sections of Central Europe as the *Harvest Home* and in others as the *Harvest Festival*, is celebrated in much the same manner as the festival of the same name in England, Scotland, and Ireland. In some sections of Czechoslovakia, the last sheaf cut and bound in the fields is called the *Baba*. This is taken in ceremonial procession back to the barn to be presented to the owner of the farm. The farmer, in turn, invites all of his helpers to a feast which they share with laughter, dancing, and rejoicing over the good harvest.[8]

---

[1]Spicer, *op. cit.*, pp. 344-345.
[2]Rearick, *op. cit.*, p. 32.
[3]Spicer, *op. cit.*, p. 296.
[4]*Ibid.*, p. 346.
[5]*Ibid.*, p. 89.
[6]Rearick, *op. cit.*, p. 37.
[7]*Ibid.*, p. 38.
[8]Spicer, *op. cit.*, p. 90.

Hungarian

Serbian

Russian and Central European

Russian

Russian

Moravian

FOUR STEPS

Four Steps is the English title for *Čtyři Kroky*, taking its name from the introductory step which is identical with the first step of the Norwegian *Rugen*. It is very similar to the German folk dance *Seven Steps* both with respect to the derivation of its title and to the general pattern of the basic steps as they are danced in a simple one-part form.

Formation: Any number of couples in a single circle, partners facing in closed social dance position, extended arms toward center of circle so that Man faces counterclockwise, Woman clockwise.

	COUNTS	MEASURES
Man begins L, Woman R, to dance		
3 slides toward center of circle	1&,2&, 1&.	
Stamp, taking weight (Man L, Woman R)	2	
Hold	&	1-2
Repeat Meas. 1 and 2, reversing feet and moving away from center of circle to original positions		3-4
1 slide toward center of circle (Man L, Woman R)	1&	
Stamp, taking weight (Man L, Woman R)	2	
Hold	&	5
1 slide away from center of circle (Man R, Woman L)	1&	
Stamp, taking weight (Man R, Woman L)	2	
Hold	&	6
Partners make one turn clockwise while progressing counterclockwise around the large circle with		
2 polka steps (Man hops lightly on R to begin, Woman hops lightly on L)	ah 1 & 2, ah 1 & 2	7-8

Repeat entire dance as many times as desired.

M.M. ♩ = 104   FOUR STEPS   *Czechoslovakia*

IN THE GREEN MEADOW

This delightful Czechoslovakian dance takes its name from the title *Na Ty Louce Zeleny* which is translated "In the Green Meadow." A one-part form, it is light and lyrical in style with step patterns which are quite similar to several of the Swiss and Bavarian dances included in this collection.

Formation: Any number of couples in a double circle facing counterclockwise, Man on L of partner, inside hands joined, outside hands on hips.

	COUNTS	MEASURES

A. Couples dance in place (Man beginning L, Woman R), with
  1 waltz balance step, turning away from each other and swinging joined hands strongly forward . . . . 1,2,3 — 1
  1 waltz balance step, turning toward each other and swinging joined hands strongly backward . . . . 1,2,3 — 2
Swinging joined hands strongly forward and upward, partners release hands and turn away from each other, making one complete turn progressing counterclockwise around the circle, finishing to face again [See Plate 5, page 49], with
  2 waltz steps (Man L, R, Woman R, L) except that the weight is not taken on the outside foot at the close of the second waltz step (Ct. 3, Meas. 4) to leave that foot free for repeating A . . — 3-4
Repeat Meas. 1-4 reversing feet and direction, beginning on outside foot (Man R, Woman L) and moving clockwise . . . . . . — 5-8

B. In a single circle, facing counterclockwise,
Woman, in front of partner with both hands on hips, dances forward, making four turns clockwise with
  8 waltz steps

while

Man follows her in a single circle progressing counterclockwise, clapping his hands on the first beat of each measure with
  8 waltz balance steps . . . . — 9-16

C. In social dance position, couples turn clockwise while progressing counterclockwise around the large circle with
  8 waltz steps . . . . — 17-24

Repeat entire dance as many times as desired.

IN THE GREEN MEADOW

Czechoslovakia

M.M. ♩ = 132

mf

CSARDAS

The *Csárdás* is the national dance of Hungary since it is the most popularly performed and universally known folk dance of this country. Like the national dances of other countries, the *Csárdás* appears in many versions with innumerable variations of the basic steps common to all sections. Also, the *Csárdás* does not actually have one established, definite sequence of steps due to the fact that the order of the characteristic steps performed in its execution is often arranged at the whim of the couple performing it, the man taking the initiative in introducing each step in turn, the woman imitating and following the steps which her partner introduces. Steps and formations are often improvised, therefore, according to the abilities and inclinations of those performing the *Csárdás*.

The significance of the title of this national dance is directly related to the fact that *Csárdá* means literally "inn" and *Csárdás* is variously translated as "inkeeper" or "affairs at the inn;" therefore, the *Csárdás* has been for many years a popular Hungarian folk dance and a favorite form of social and couple dance for those who gathered in the inns for recreation during their leisure hours. In Hungary it is danced in two distinct parts. The first part is relatively slow in tempo and the movements so executed that head and torso swing rhythmically from side to side in a somewhat horizontal plane in the direction of the steps initiated by the movements of the feet. The second part is faster in tempo and more spirited in style, characterized by jumping and hopping steps, with the alignment of the body more vertical than horizontal. This distinction between the two parts of the *Csárdás* with respect to tempi and mood has given rise to confusion in references to *slow* and *fast* dances bearing the same title of *Csárdás*. This may be due in part to the fact that Hungarian peasants use the terms *slow dance* and *quick dance* in referring to the two parts of the *Csárdás* although the two parts constitute this national dance as a whole. They use these terms in requesting music from native orchestras and often two different pieces of music—one slow, one fast—are played as accompaniment.

The version of the *Csárdás* presented in this unit of the present collection of folk dances is sometimes called the *Ballroom Csárdás* and is not divided into the two distinct parts which Hungarian peasants designate as a *slow* and *quick* dance comprising the *Csárdás* as a whole.

Formation: Any number of couples in a single circle, partners facing directly in shoulder-waist position, Man facing counterclockwise, Woman clockwise. Man begins L, Woman R. Man's part is analyzed; Woman's is opposite with a reversal of feet and directions throughout.

	COUNTS	MEASURES
A. All dance toward center of circle with		
Step to L side	1	
Close R to L, taking weight R	&	
Step L to side	2	
Close R to L, at same time rising slightly on balls of feet, toes inverted to click heels together sharply	&	1
Repeat Meas. 1 seven times, beginning R and alternately stepping sideward to R and L, respectively		2-8

COUNTS   MEASURES

B. Retaining shoulder-waist position, partners make a quarter-turn L, so that they are side by side in a single circle, Man facing in, Woman out. [See Hungarian couple on Russian and Central European Costume Plate for position of partners.] Pulling away from each other in this position, partners make two clockwise turns in place, both beginning R, with

Step forward R, bending R knee sharply 1

Step forward L, rising on ball of L foot close to R . . . . &

Repeat 7 times to complete two clockwise turns, omitting last step L . . . . 2&, etc.   9-12

Partners reverse starting position with a sharp half-turn to the R, bringing L hips and shoulders toward each other so that Man now faces out of the circle, Woman toward the center and repeat Meas. 1-4, beginning L, making 2 counterclockwise turns in place, Woman freeing R foot to repeat dance 13-16

Variation

This same turn in place may be executed with the following variation in step pattern:

Beginning L, partners make two clockwise turns in place with

Step forward L 1

Step forward R . . . . &

Hop R . . . . ah

Repeat 7 times, omitting last step and hop R . . . . . 2&, ah, etc.   9-12

Partners reverse position and, beginning R, make two counterclockwise turns in place with the same step, omitting last step and hop L, leaving L foot free to repeat dance. Woman frees R foot to repeat dance 13-16

Repeat entire dance as many times as desired.

CSARDAS

Hungary

CSEBOGAR

Csébogar is a popular Hungarian folk dance with some of the same basic steps which characterize the *Csárdás*, the national dance of Hungary. Its two main figures follow the two-part form of the folk tune to which it is danced, each concluded with the spirited Hungarian turn.

Formation: Any number of couples in a single circle facing in, Man on L of partner, with all hands joined.

I

	COUNTS	MEASURES
A. All move clockwise around the circle with		
Hop R	ah	
8 sliding steps, beginning L, keeping R foot free on last step .	1, ah 2, ah 1, ah 2, etc.	1-4
Repeat, beginning with a hop L and moving counterclockwise .		5-8
B. All move forward toward center of circle, beginning L, with		
4 skip steps		1-2
All move backward to places, beginning L, with		
4 skip steps		3-4

Releasing hands, Men face toward center of circle, Women away from center so that R sides of bodies are turned toward each other, R feet close together, R arms around each other's waists, L arms curved overhead. [See Hungarian couple on Russian and Central European Costume Plate for position of partners, noting that L arms are curved overhead in *Csébogar*.] Couples make two clockwise turns in place leaning strongly away from each other but keeping R hips and feet close together with

	COUNTS	MEASURES
Hop R	ah	
Step L	1	
Step R in place	2	5
Repeat 3 times, Women omitting last step R to free R foot for beginning of Figure II	ah 1,2, ah 1,2, etc.	6-8 2nd ending

II

A. In shoulder-waist position, partners facing in a single circle, Man beginning L, Woman R, all move sideward toward center of circle. (Man's part is analyzed; Woman's is opposite with a reversal of feet and directions throughout)

	COUNTS	MEASURES
Step L	1	
Close R to L, taking weight	2	9
Repeat 3 times, keeping R free on last close step	1,2,1,2, etc.	10-12
Repeat all, Man beginning R, Woman L, moving sideward away from center of circle to original places		13-16

COUNTS   MEASURES

B. All move sideward toward center of circle, Man beginning L, Woman R. (Man's part is analyzed; Woman's is opposite with a reversal of feet and directions throughout)

Step L 1

Close R to L, taking weight 2

Step L 1

Close R to L, without taking weight 2   9-10

Repeat, moving sideward away from center of circle to original places. Women take weight R on last close step   11-12

Repeat Hungarian turn as analyzed for Meas. 5-8 in B of Figure I, finishing with stamp of L foot on Ct. 1 of Meas. 16 and shout on Ct. 2 of Meas. 16   13-16

HANDKERCHIEF DANCE

The *Handkerchief Dance*, known in Moravia as *Sátečková*, takes its name from the fact that partners grasp the corners of handkerchiefs held by both hands between them. Part I is danced in triple meter, using a running waltz step while Part II is danced in duple meter with a polka. In keeping with the contrast between these parts, the style for dancing the first part should be smooth and flowing and that for the second staccato and spirited.

Formation: Any number of couples in a single circle facing counterclockwise, Woman in front of Man, with handkerchiefs held by the corners in their R and L hands, so that Woman's arms are bent at the elbows, Man's extended forward, handkerchiefs at shoulder level.

I

COUNTS   MEASURES

Dancers move counterclockwise around the circle (beginning R), both arms raised upward and sideward, with

8 running waltz steps, the Woman looking alternately over her R and L shoulders at the Man who progresses slightly to the side on alternate steps so as to look at the Woman over her shoulders. [See Moravian couple on Russian and Central European Costume Plate.] 1,2,3,   1-8
etc.

CSEBOGAR

Hungary

II

	COUNTS	MEASURES

With handkerchiefs raised high overhead (keeping them taut and parallel) dancers turn to Man's R, Woman's L (both beginning L) under their joined arms while progressing counterclockwise in a large circle with

8 light polka steps (L, R, L, R, etc.) . . . .   ah 1&2, etc.   9-16

Repeat, reversing the direction of the turn under the joined arms to Man's L, Woman's R continuing to progress counterclockwise around the circle. [See Plate 9] . . . .   9-16 repeated

Repeat entire dance as many times as desired.

HANDKERCHIEF DANCE

Moravia

M.M. ♩ = 132

Plate 9

Handkerchief Dance

113

KANAFASKA

Kanafaska is a particularly interesting Moravian dance in that it is executed in a square or quadrille formation common to the folk dances of many countries and a predecessor, therefore, of our popular American square dances. The dance is a lively two-part form.

Formation: Any number of sets of four couples in a square, Man on L of partner, with couples numbered 1, 2, 3 and 4, respectively, in a counterclockwise direction around the square [See Diagram 13].

I

	COUNTS	MEASURES
In social dance position, clasped hands extended sideward at shoulder level toward center of square, Man beginning L, Woman R, Couples 1 and 3 exchange places, Men passing back to back, turning L in opposite position in order to place Woman on R side, with 8 sliding steps	1&, etc.	1-4
Couples 2 and 4 exchange places in same manner		5-8
Couples 1 and 3 return to original positions in same manner . .		1-4
Couples 2 and 4 return to original positions in same manner . .		5-8

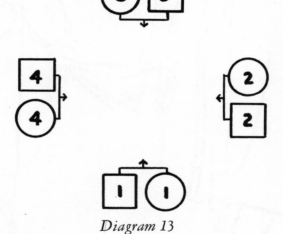

Diagram 13

II

A. Man of Couple 1, beginning L, and Woman of Couple 2, beginning R, move forward toward each other, Man clapping hands on first count, with

	COUNTS	MEASURES
2 walking steps	1,2	9
In shoulder-waist position, the two dancers turn clockwise while progressing counterclockwise in a circle within the square, dancing once around, with 6 polka steps (Man beginning with hop R, Woman L) . . .	ah 1&2, etc.	10-15

		COUNTS	MEASURES

Man lifts Woman in "toss-up" and leaves her in her original place. Woman helps to gain elevation by bending knees and pressing down upon Man's shoulders, straightening her arms as he lifts her into the air (Ct. 1&). Woman lands in position on R of Partner (Ct. 2) 1,2   16

B. Man of Couple 1 and Woman of Couple 3 dance Meas. 9-16 as described   9-16

C. Man of Couple 1 and Woman of Couple 4 dance Meas. 9-16 as described   9-16

D. In shoulder-waist position, partners turn clockwise while progressing once around in a complete counterclockwise circle to finish in original starting position with
    8 polka steps (Man beginning with hop R, Woman L).
        Couples 1 and 3 and Couples 2 and 4 remain opposite each other throughout   9-16

Repeat Figure I as analyzed 1-8, 1-8

Repeat Figure II, Man 2 dancing in turn with Women 3, 4, 1 and 2 .   9-16
                                                        4 times

Repeat Figure I as analyzed 1-8, 1-8

Repeat Figure II, Man 3 dancing in turn with Women 4, 1, 2 and 3 .   9-16
                                                        4 times

Repeat Figure I as analyzed 1-8, 1-8

Repeat Figure II, Man 4 dancing in turn with Women 1, 2, 3 and 4 .   9-16
                                                        4 times

KANAFASKA

M.M. ♩ = 120

Moravia

Play 4 times to next double bar

rall------

115

KOROBOUSHKA

Koróboushka means literally "Peddler's Pack" and may be classified broadly, therefore, as an occupational dance commemorating this colorful trade common the world over. The movements of the dance bear but faint resemblance to the significance of the title except that they entail an "exchange" of places and of positions of partners when danced as a "mixer."

According to some authorities, *Koróboushka* is not danced generally in Russia but has evolved, more or less, among Russian immigrants in this country. If this is true, it is nevertheless an authentic Russian folk dance although its origin is more recent than ancient.

Like many folk dances, there are several versions and many variations of *Koróboushka*, all of which, however, use the same melody in duple meter and are executed in a spirited, vigorous manner. Two popular versions are described here with differences confined primarily to the formation or design of the dance as a whole—sometimes performed in a longways set and sometimes in a double circle introducing the progression of partners in the latter. *Koróboushka* is an excellent "mixer" with which to begin folk dance parties, based upon Slavic themes, when it is danced in the circular and progressive fashion.

The dance is a one-part form with changing step patterns in keeping with the changing phrases in the musical accompaniment to which it is danced.

Version I

Formation: Any number of couples in a longways set, Man on the L, partners facing with straight arms extended forward at shoulder level, both hands joined.

	COUNTS	MEASURES
A. Both dancers move toward R wall, Man beginning L and moving forward, Woman beginning R and moving backward, with		
3 walking steps (Man L, R, L, Woman R, L, R)	1,2,1	
Hop on firm foot, swinging free foot slightly forward (Man hops L, Woman R)	2	1-2
Repeat Meas. 1 and 2, reversing feet and directions, so that Man moves backward toward L wall, Woman forward		3-4
Repeat Meas. 1 and 2 as analyzed		5-6
Man moves backward, Woman forward, with		
Step (Man R, Woman L)	1	
Hop on firm foot (Man R, Woman L) pointing free foot to side, toes touching floor (Man L, Woman R)	2	7
Hop on firm foot bringing feet together, weight on balls of both feet, clicking heels together	1	
Hold	2	8
B. Releasing joined hands and placing both hands on hips, all dance sideward to the R, with		
Step sideward R	1	
Step L across just in back of R	2	9
Step sideward R	1	

	COUNTS	MEASURES
Hop R, at same time swinging L foot diagonally forward across in front of R	2	10
Repeat Meas. 9 and 10 moving to L, reversing feet and directions .		11-12
Joining R hands, free hands on hips, partners		
Step R toward each other	1	
Hop R, swinging L slightly forward	2	13
Step backward L	1	
Hop L, swinging R slightly forward	2	14
Partners exchange places in original longways set passing by R shoulders with		
3 walking steps (R, L, R)	1,2,1	
Bring feet together, clicking heels	2	15-16
Repeat Meas. 9-16, partners facing, with Men on the R and Women on the L of the original longways set of two parallel columns, reversing feet and directions throughout so that dancers finish in their original starting positions. All begin L and move to L . .		9-16 repeated

Repeat entire dance as many times as desired.

Version II

If *Koróboushka* is danced in a circle with progressive design, it begins with a double circle for any number of couples, partners facing with both hands joined, Man's back to the center of the circle. The steps are identical with those described in *Version I*. In this version of *Koróboushka*, the A part begins with the Man moving forward away from the center of the circle, Woman backward. The progression takes place as partners release joined hands and each Man progresses with the last three walking steps (Meas. 15–16) counterclockwise around the original circle, joining hands with the next Woman who becomes his partner for the repetition of the dance as a whole.

KOROBOUSHKA   *Russia*

IN THE GARDEN

This typical Russian dance may be classified broadly as an occupational dance associated originally with gardening or farming activities although its steps bear few if any literal resemblances to occupational dances as such. This particular folk dance was originally performed by either men or women alone rather than by mixed groups. While the dance is recorded in a definite sequence of established steps, we are told that originally a leader in the center of the circular formation introduced the combination of basic steps in whatever order he or she chose, the group following in the execution of the steps thus combined. The dance seems highly appropriate for a group of girls or women.

In the Garden should be danced in a vigorous, spirited fashion with sharply accented steps wherever indicated. The changes in the rhythmic patterns of the various steps in each figure introduce interesting and contrasting sound patterns.

Formation: A single circle of any number of Women (or Men) all facing inward toward center of circle, R hand curved overhead holding handkerchief, L hand on hip, knuckles to the hip. [See Russian Woman on Russian and Central European Costume Plate.] The handkerchief should be flourished with the accents of each measure in A and F.

		COUNTS	MEASURES
A.	All move sideward in counterclockwise circle, beginning R, with		
	Stamp R to side, at same time cutting L slightly but sharply to L	1	
	Step L close to R heel	&	
	Repeat 13 times, continuing to move sideward R in a counterclockwise circle, stamping on the R and pushing with the ball of the L foot	2&, etc.	1-7
	Stamp R to side	1	
	Step L beside R	2	8
B.	Placing both hands on hips, each dancer moves in a small clockwise circle, aligning the circumference of the individual circles with dancers on the R and L, respectively [See Diagram 14, page 120], with 8 polka steps, beginning with slight hop L	ah 1&2, etc.	9-16
C.	In a single circle, facing counterclockwise, dancers move forward in line of direction, both arms raised shoulder high, arms curved inward overhead, palms facing, with		
	Step R forward	1	
	Close L to R, taking weight L	&	
	Stamp R, at same time cutting L foot forward and off floor (hips tucked under) and bending upper body to L	2	
	Hold	&	17
	Repeat 7 times, beginning alternately L, R, L, etc., facing center of circle on end of last step		18-24
D.	In a single circle, facing in, R hand curved overhead holding handkerchief, L hand on hip, all dance in place with		
	Step R over L, swinging R leg in wide arc in front from R to L before taking weight R, bending both knees deeply	1	

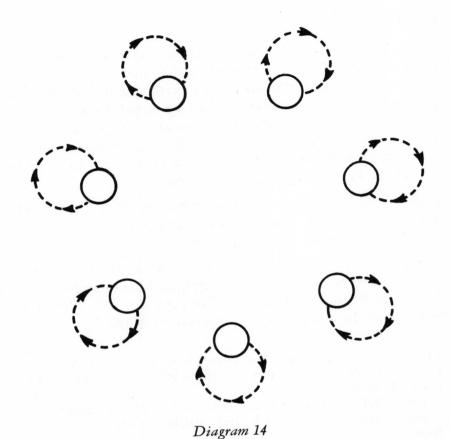

Diagram 14

	COUNTS	MEASURES
Step L directly backward	2	25
Step R to side	1	
Step L across in front of R	2	26

Repeat Meas. 1 and 2 three times, always swinging R leg in wide arc to step across in front of L on first count with twist of body from R to L and deep bend of R knee as weight is taken on R foot. [See Diagram 15] 27-32

E. In a single circle facing clockwise, both hands on hips, all dance backward in a counterclockwise direction with
8 polka steps, beginning with slight hop on L 33-40

F. In a single circle, facing in, all dance sideward counterclockwise with
41-47
14 steps as analyzed in A . . . .
Stamp R to side 1
Stamp L beside R, shouting "Hey," holding final flourish of handkerchief overhead 2 48

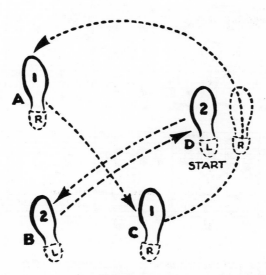

Diagram 15

IN THE GARDEN

Russia

KOLO

Because the *Kolo* is the favorite and most universally popular dance of Serbia, it may be designated as the national dance of this particular country. Like the national dances of all countries, it has many variations. The word *Kolo* is thought to be a derivative of a Slavic word meaning "chain" — hence, the significance of the Serbian dance of this title since it is performed by a chain of dancers as described in the formation below.

The basic steps of the *Kolo* are described here and afford a satisfying and authentic pattern for their execution. In its performance by skillful Serbian dancers, these basic steps are "embroidered" with an intricacy of "footwork" that does not lend itself to descriptive analysis. The basic steps, however, are fundamental and authentic and may be executed with complete confidence and satisfaction as they have been performed satisfactorily by the authors with skillful Serbian dancers despite the fact that these particular dancers "embroidered" the basic steps thus analyzed with extra flourishes of the free foot.

The *Kolo* is a simple one-part form involving frequent change of direction with changing phrases. It should be danced in a lively fashion. Women should keep bodies erect to avoid sagging on Men's shoulders, thus causing the dance to move heavily. Dancers must gauge length of steps and space in travelling so that the entire line of performers moves smoothly.

Formation: The *Kolo* may be danced by any number of couples in a single line, a circle, or by two parallel lines facing. It may be danced either by couples or by groups of Men or Women linked together by joined hands. If performed by couples in two parallel lines facing, as presented here, Men are on the L of their partners, R and L arms around the waists of the Women on their R and L, respectively, while the Women place their hands on the shoulders of the Men on either side. The dancers on the end of each of the two parallel lines place their outside hands on the hips, fingers to the front. All begin with the L foot and the two lines advance forward toward each other and sideward as indicated. [For formation used in this version of *Kolo* see Diagram 16].

	COUNTS	MEASURES
All dance forward, beginning L with 4 small running steps (L, R, L, R)	1,2,3,4	1
All dance backward, beginning L with 4 small running steps (L, R, L, R)	1,2,3,4	2
All dance sideward to the L with Step L to side	1	

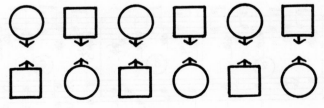

Diagram 16

	COUNTS	MEASURES
Step R across just in back of L	2	
Step L to side	3	
Hop L, swinging R diagonally forward and across in front of L .	4	3
Repeat Meas. 3, moving sideward to the R and reversing feet and directions		4
All dance in place with		
Stamp L to side	1	
Hop L, swinging R diagonally forward and across in front of L .	2	
Stamp R to side	3	
Hop R, swinging L diagonally forward and across in front of R .	4	5
Repeat movements of Meas. 5	1-4	6
Move sideward L with		
Stamp L to side	1	
Step R just in back of L	2	
Stamp L to side	3	
Step R just in back of L	4	7
Stamp L to side	1	
Step R just in back of L	2	
Stamp L to side	3	
Hop L, swinging R diagonally forward and across in front of L .	4	8
Repeat Meas. 7 and 8, moving sideward to the R and reversing feet and directions		9-10
Repeat all two times, accelerating the tempo with each repetition so that dancers are moving as rapidly as possible on the third performance of the dance which is often finished with the shouting of "Hey!"		1-10
		1-10

KOLO

Serbia

M.M. ♩ = 132

FOLK DANCES OF FRANCE

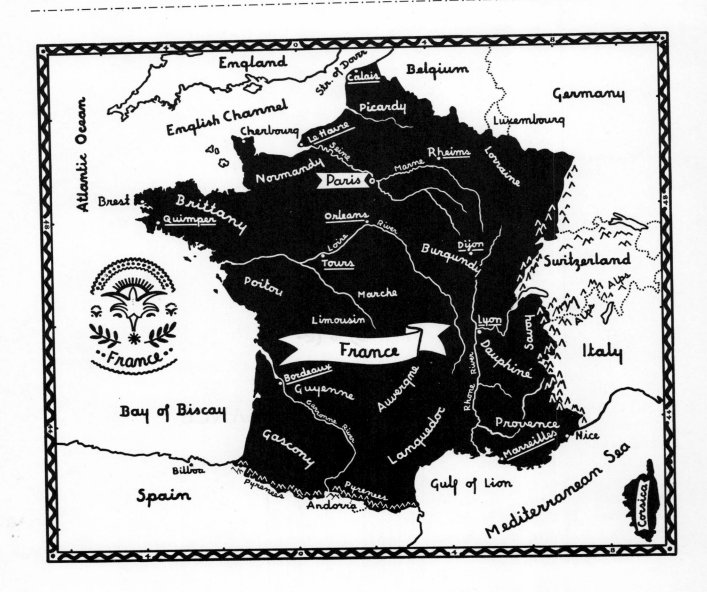

France

GEOGRAPHICAL BACKGROUND

The Republic of France constitutes an area of 212,659 square miles which links the Iberian Peninsula to the body of Europe, and is slightly smaller in size than the combined areas of New Mexico and Colorado. France is bounded on the east by Belgium, Luxembourg, Germany, Switzerland and Italy, on the north by the English channel which separates France from the British Isles, on the west by the Bay of Biscay, and on the south by Spain and the Mediterranean Sea.

The coastal areas of France are only slightly above sea level, forming lowland regions. The winds which blow from the south and west onto these low sections are gentle and therefore provide a warm, mild climate with generous annual rainfall. Central France is a higher plateau area with a broken terrain across which chilly winds blow resulting in especially bleak winters. From the plateau up to the mountains of Southern and Southeastern France are the highlands of this country. Along the border between Spain and France is the almost impregnable mountainous barrier formed by the Pyrenees with a rugged, austere landscape accented by snow-capped peaks. Southeastern France is covered with the western range of Alps which form a barrier between that country and Switzerland and Italy. Cutting through the Alps across the southeastern corner of France is the rich valley formed by the Rhone River. Along the Mediterranean coast of the country is an expanse of land swept by the soft, warm breezes of the sea known as the French Riviera, a famous vacation resort of the world.

France is known, primarily, as an agricultural country and the French people as industrious, progressive farmers. The foremost crop cultivated in France is the grapevine, yielding the finest quality and a large portion of the quantity of wines produced the world over. Second in importance to the vineyards is the cultivation of cereal grains—wheat, oats, barley, and rye. Along the Mediterranean coast are citrus fruit orchards; apples and nuts are grown in large quantities in Northern France. Because of its extensive coastal areas, France has a large fishing industry with fleets which go quite far out to sea and even into the northern waters. Most important of France's manufactured products are her textiles with silk first and fine woolens and cottons next in importance.

HISTORICAL AND SOCIOLOGICAL BACKGROUND

The earliest record of the people living in the section of Europe now known as France is the account written by Caesar about ancient Gaul. In 58 B. C., he led his armies northwestward across the Alps and waged an eight-year battle with the Celtic peoples he found living there. As he won victories over them, he began his Romanization of these new lands. By the close of the fourth century, the Celts had accepted the new civilization and had adopted the Christian religion. During the following century, fierce Teutonic tribes from the north and northeast pushed down through France—the Visigoths who settled Southwestern France, the Burgundians who settled in Southern France, and the Franks who settled in Northern France —driving the original Celtic tribes into the central part of what was then known as Gaul. In 451 A.D., these recent barbaric inhabitants were forced to join with the Christianized Celts under Roman rule to repulse a Mongolian invasion from the East led by Attila. The famous Battle of Chalons marked the turning point of this campaign, resulting in the expulsion of the orientals from Western Europe and the preservation of the country for a Western culture.

During the fifth century, a young Frankish king named Clovis began to develop greater armies and subsequent power until, in the latter part of the century, he overthrew the Roman ruler of Gaul, subdued the Visigothic powers and became ruler of all of Gaul. As a Christian convert, he was acceptable to the Celts as a ruler whereas they would not have submitted to the rule of a barbarian. Thus France, deriving its name from "the Frankish kingdom," came into being. By the middle of the seventh century, the descendants of Clovis, the Merovingian king of France, had become ineffective as rulers and France was again in need of a leader. Pippin of Heristal, as an official in the government, gained control of the kingdom and laid the foundation for the subsequent transfer of rule from the Merovingians to the Carolingians.

During the Carolingian Dynasty, the French protected Europe from an invasion of the Moors by driving them out of France in the Battle of Tours in 732. The Norsemen, or Normans, landed on the northern coast of France and, to prevent their further inroads into this country, were given the section of land which we know now as Normandy. Charlemagne, with the idea of extending his own government to all of Europe and thus establishing a consolidated Christian empire, pushed with his armies in all directions and, in 800, was crowned Emperor of the West by Pope Leo III. With the death of Charlemagne, the empire collapsed. The division of the lands of Europe into the countries now known as France, Germany, and Italy gradually took place and the social system later known as feudalism began its development. By the close of the tenth century, the Carolingian Dynasty had weakened and France again was in need of leadership. A duke, Hugh Capet, succeeded in overthrowing the king of those lands then known as France and founded the Capetian Dynasty which ruled, either directly or from one of its branches, until the time of the French Revolution.

The Hundred Years' War in France, 1337-1378 and 1413-1453, involved conflicts at home between political groups as well as war with England. Then followed the religious wars between the Catholics and Protestants, or Huguenots, which were ended when Henry IV of Navarre, leader of the Protestants, reached the throne, accepted Roman Catholicism as his religion, and granted religious liberty to the Protestants with his famous Edict of Nantes (1598).

The crown of France became more and more absolute with each succeeding king until the luxury-loving and licentious courts of Louis' XIV, XV, and XVI reached their heights of elegance. The people, at first impressed with the grandeur of the French Court and of the nobility, soon realized that they provided, through heavy taxations, the funds which were flowing down a frivolous drain. In 1789, the King, aware of the growing unrest, summoned the Parliament. In the first meeting, the spirit of revolt on the part of the bourgeois was apparent. The few years that followed were stormy ones, culminating in the French Revolution with subsequent freedom and liberties for the masses. This restless period included a Reign of Terror and civil war within France and wars with several neighboring countries.

As is so often the case, the men who seized the control of the French government at the time of the Revolution were ambitious and sought personal power, introducing into the government abuses which were equal to those suffered by the people under their previous kings. This gave the royalists opportunity to plot a counter-revolution. The people of the country were eager for any alternative at this juncture of their history and in 1804, they established an empire with an hereditary government, naming Napoleon Bonaparte as emperor.

Napoleon launched his famous campaign which extended the French Empire over most of Europe. In 1812, when he started with his armies in an attempt to storm Moscow, his over-ambitious career collapsed. He was driven back across Europe to Paris where he abdicated in 1814. At this point, Talleyrand, a French political leader, recommended that the Bourbons be recalled and Louis XVIII was crowned king of France. Thirty-four years later, the people, convinced anew of their exploitation by the French monarchists, banished the king and established a second republic, electing the nephew of the great Napoleon, Louis Napoleon or Napoleon III, as president. He, however, proved personally ambitious and sought more than a mere presidency. By 1852, he had gained sufficient power to have himself named emperor, and the Second Empire of France was launched. The development of Prussian power during the next few years was watched by all of Europe, and especially by France, with a growing feeling of anxiety. In 1870, France and Prussia engaged in a war which resulted in a defeat for France and the subsequent loss of all of her European empire, including the provinces of Alsace and Lorraine. When news of the defeat reached the French people, Napoleon III was removed as emperor and France again established a republic — the Third Republic — electing Adolphe Thiers as its president. Between 1871 and 1914 France aligned herself with several European powers in an effort to check German expansion.

In 1914 France was plunged once more into a war with Germany and at the close of the first World War, in which England and later the United States entered on the side of France, she regained Alsace and Lorraine. Twenty-five years later, after a time of continual internal dissension, France was invaded by German troups under Adolf Hitler, dictator of Germany. In this second world conflict England and the United States joined forces against Germany and, ultimately, with the assistance of Russia and other allies, finally defeated the German troops. The Nazi occupation and the Hitler-inspired Vichy Government collapsed. Today the Republic of France is again a free country with her lands divided for purposes of political organization into eighty-nine departments (including the island of Corsica) rather than into the original provinces. Her present total population numbers 41,980,000 people.

France has long been known as a cultural center of world-wide influence. Many of her artists, composers, philosophers, and scientists have been in the front ranks of achievement. Contributions made by some of the most famous persons of France include Montaigne, Descartes, and Voltaire in philosophy; Corot and Delacroix in painting; Rodin in sculpture; Curie and Pasteur in science; Hugo, Dumas, Zola, and Proust in literature; and Racine in drama.

FOLK DANCES

It is somewhat startling to discover that France, the home of a race peculiarly sensitive to beauty and aesthetic appreciations, developed relatively few folk dances and no real national dance in contrast to the abundance of those evolved by her more stolid neighbors in many other countries. Contrary to expectations, France offers one of the more meager heritages in this particular area of folk culture. Dance historians give two general explanations for this enigma. First, they reason that people who toil long hours at confining and exacting work crave, in their leisure time, a form of activity which will release the mind from any demands of attention and that only one type of folk dance can evolve from such a people — a folk dance devoid of intricate steps and figures. France serves as an admirable illustration of this viewpoint voiced by the Kinneys when they state that "The people of the country are, first of all, workers, the dances that enliven their fêtes are the careless celebration of children released from confining tasks."[1] Thus, each small section of France has developed numerous simple, short dances closely associated with the leisure hours of the particular group from which they arose. The second reason for the generalization that France, as a country, offers comparatively little as a heritage in folk dances is closely related to the first. Folk dance is the dance of the peasantry, passed on from generation to generation without the aid of professional teachers and performers. The French people as a race are artistic and innately endowed with the potentiality for expressing their love of beauty through superb skills and elaborate decorativeness. The kind of labor in which the common people have always engaged offered little opportunity for such aesthetic satisfactions. Their neighbors, the Spanish, another group of Latin people, also possess a sensitiveness to beauty as a national trait. With the Spanish, however, this desire for refinement of beauty, coupled with the leisure for which they provide, has resulted in a particularly elaborate and refined type of folk dance in Spain. The French, on the other hand, being of a thrifty nature, direct most of their energies into labor which has remunerative value and therefore do not have time left for developing a form of dance which can satisfy their tastes for artistic movement. For this reason, the folk dances of the masses of French people remain for the most part simple, frolicsome forms of play. To satisfy the finer urge for artistic dance, the French developed opera ballets in the principal cities and sponsored the growth of the ballet as an art form.[2] The leisure class in the French Courts of pre-Revolution days developed the simple folk dance forms of the people into elaborate, refined dances which represent the zenith of perfection in detail and structure.

For purposes of an overview, the folk dances of France may be divided into two broad categories — those ceremonial and ritualistic in their implications and those folk dances enjoyed by all for purposes of recreation and amusement on any social occasion. The folk dances included in this collection represent the latter type. For the most part, they reflect the earlier influences of primitive religious dances of France; they are characterized by a quaint combination of stately decorum and dignity and a gay spirit of free, relaxed play.

---

[1]Kinney, *op. cit.*, p. 183.
[2]*Ibid.*, p. 165.

The ceremonial medicine dances, used by primitive man to drive from the infirm the spirit of sickness, were danced in France, according to Sachs, as late as the end of the ninetenth century.[1] The primitive ceremonial fertility rites, for the purpose of invoking the blessing of nature upon the crops, were performed in France sometimes by priests, sometimes by peasants, and sometimes by processions of both. These dances — closely related to those of England and other countries — involved the circling of the dancers about a pole decorated with grain, fruit, flowers, and colored ribbons, or about a living tree which was hallowed as a fertility center. The farmers of central France performed arch and bridge dances — characterized by having one couple make an arch of their joined hands under which other couples passed — as a part of their fertility rites in the belief that the hemp would grow better following their perform-ance.[2] Sachs points out further that "From the fertility dances stems the famous *carmagnole* — the round dance of the French Revolution around the tree of liberty and the guillotine."[3] The *carmagnole* derives its name from the city of Carmagnola in Piedmont. The dance itself is sometimes called the *carmagnola*. Suspending a cap of liberty on the top of a tree, the dancers move wildly and triumphantly about it.

Religious dances — very prevalent among the French people — were performed throughout the Middle Ages at the feasts of patron saints and on the eve of great church festivals.[4] The *Pardon-Dantza* danced on the Feast of St. John — a slow and languishing ceremonial folk dance — may be classified in this religious group. Urlin gives us a vivid description of the *Edate*, a ceremonial dance organized in every village in Guipuzcoa by the Alcalde.[5] The girls drew together after church on Sunday and dared their lovers to fight. The men joined them in a solemn sort of processional which changed to brisk and whirling movements at a signal given by the Alcalde. Throughout the dance the women's part predominates, since the women serve as leaders of the men.

Many of the dances from the people of Brittany can be traced back to the nature-worship of their Celtic ancestry.[6] These particular dances were performed on Saturday afternoons in June of each year around the dolmens or tomb-like monuments. The girls decorated their hats with the blossoms of the flax while the boys wore the green heads of the wheat. Some of the dances which followed bore a quaint resemblance to American quadrilles with a musician in the center who called out the figures.

Urlin[7] stresses the importance of ceremonial folk dances as a part of the religious life of the Bretons in conjunction with their Pardons and other church festivals. The tolling of the church bells sound first, followed by Mass. The statues of the saints, decorated and dressed in national costumes, receive offerings of flax, corn, cakes and sheepskins. These rituals are followed by folk dancing around the dolmen, — dancing which is both gay and grave. The music is played on the *binyou*, — a sort of bagpipe used widely for folk song and dance in

[1]Sachs, *op. cit.*, p. 63.
[2]*Ibid.*, p. 163.
[3]*Ibid.*, p. 65.
[4]Gaston Vuillier, *A History of Dancing* (New York: D. Appleton-Century Company, 1897), p. 60.
[5]Urlin, *op. cit.*, p. 72.
[6]*Ibid.*, p. 114.
[7]*Ibid.*, p. 41.

Brittany and in other areas of France. The melodies used for accompaniment have their origin in the Greek modes and are similar in sound to Plain-song and Gregorian chants.

Marriage rites in all countries have been accompanied by special ceremonial dances as well as by the general social dancing of all present. From this folk custom, doubtless, we derive our everyday adage of "I'll dance at your wedding." Sometimes the bride, sometimes the groom, and sometimes both as well as others in attendance at the celebration of this sacred rite perform the ceremonial marriage dances. The marriage dances take various forms in different countries. Charms for strength and fertility are woven into their performance. Encircling some object symbolic of these attributes or related to the newly acquired marital state is a significant aspect of the marriage folk dances.[1] Three is a favorite number of times designated for these circumambulations. The number "three" has been associated with charms throughout folklore,—hence our own common saying "The third time is the charm." Young French girls, particularly of Ille-Et-Vilaine, who wish to marry, dance three times around a bramble of three branches. The newly married couple in Auvergne dance three times around the dolmens or sacred stones as a part of the marriage rites.

The foregoing will suffice to illustrate France's contributions to the ceremonial folk dances of the world. In the field of social folk dances, two French dances are referred to most frequently by all dance historians, namely the *bourrée* and the *farandole*. The *bourrée*—one of the most vigorous of the old dance forms—derives its name from the word meaning "a bundle of small pieces of wood." Horst believes the dance to have evolved from an ancient Gallic festival—the "Jour des Fagots" during which the Gauls, with flaming torches, danced about huge bonfires.[2] The *bourrée*, a rustic sort of clog or step dance, is popular in the mountainous provinces of Auvergne and Berri in central France. Courtship is the theme of this particular folk dance. The man in each couple stamps, claps, and shouts with the woman becoming alternately bold and shy in her coquetry. The couples mix and cross, snapping their fingers and beating out the fascinating rhythmic patterns of the *bourrée* with their feet. The human voice, the bagpipes, or a sort of hurdy-gurdy furnish the musical accompaniment. The *bourrée* is sometimes danced to establish a rhythmic labor pattern for the barefooted winemakers who crush the grapes by their stamping and vigorous dancing as they sing.

The *farandole* is scarcely more than a romping and rollicking game of "follow the leader." Very popular in the southern part of France, the *farandole* is danced by a chain of boys and girls, sometimes holding brightly colored handkerchiefs between them. A leader follows his own inclination in traversing the streets, leading the long chain of dancers in spiral, zigzag, and serpentine patterns. At intervals the first couple may form an arch under which the other dancers pass. This use of the arch, circular and serpentine figures in the *farandole* denotes its probable ultimate origin in pagan religious fertility rites of an ancient period.[3]

Other popular folk dances used for social purposes in France include the *branles* and simple *gavottes*. Most of the *branles* are slow and stately although some may be danced to a

---

[1]Sachs, *op. cit.*, p. 72-73.
[2]Horst, Louis. *Pre-Classic Dance Forms* (New York: The Dance Observer, 1937), p. 100.
[3]Vuillier, *op. cit.*, p. 226.

quickened tempo. The simple step patterns repeat themselves again and again. The designs remain primarily at the caprice of the first dancer in the line who leads his chain of dancers about the room. The *branles*, first danced in single file, later became couple dances with the introduction of more elaborate steps and designs. *Branle Gascon*, included in the present collection, illustrates the *branle* which begins slowly and gradually increases in tempo. The *gavotte* derives its name from the Gavots with whom it originated. These natives of Gap in the Upper Alps developed the *gavotte* originally as a dance of courtship and injected the kissing and capering associated with lovemaking. In Brittany, it was known as the *Gavotte Bretonne*. Endless processions of dancers, dancing the *gavotte* with whole-hearted enthusiasm, filled the squares and streets of Brittany during the marriage season.[1] Included in this collection and illustrative of the *gavotte* from Brittany are *Gavotte de Pont-Aven* and *Gavotte de Quimper*.

The *rigaudon* was originally a French peasant dance of Provence and Languedoc although some authorities attribute its origin to Italy. It was, however, a favorite among the social folk dances of France and was sung and danced to the accompaniment of tambourines.

The *passepied*, the *branle of Brittany*, also had the name *trihoris*.[2] Its movements, quick and rhythmical, were danced to a triple beat, a sort of lively minuet. The people of France, in their social gatherings, also danced the *contredanse*, *cotillion*, and *volte*, or waltz.

FOLK COSTUMES

For many years, Paris has been known as the fashion center of the world. The French artistic flair for dress has merited for her people a position of leadership in the sophisticated cities of the globe. Frenchmen in the cities of France wear much the same type of everyday costume as the urban folk of London or New York with the exception, perhaps, of the characteristic smocks and dark berets of students, shopkeepers, and clerks.

The French farmer in the rural areas of France on week-days wears a dark hat, or more often a cap, a rough shirt open at the neck, dark trousers, leather or canvas leggings to keep his trousers out of the soil, and high-top shoes or knee-boots into which the trouser legs may be stuffed. He also wears a large leather apron to protect his clothing as much as possible. The women in rural districts wear a scarf over the head, a simple blouse, a very full gathered or pleated skirt, and high-topped shoes. In the particular sections of Brittany and Normandy the farmers and working people wear sabots or wooden shoes.

On Sundays and special festival days, however, French peasants dress up in their best clothes and make quite a fine showing. Although in many sections of France the traditional colorful peasant dress is gradually being replaced by attire which more closely resembles that worn in the cities, many sections still retain the holiday apparel which closely resembles the traditional folk costumes of former decades.

As in other European countries, the folk costumes differ in the various provinces. One of the chief distinctions between the costumes which represent the different provinces of France lies in the headgear of both men and women. The women of the northern provinces, especially

[1] Horst, *op. cit.*, p. 89.
[2] *Ibid.*, p. 119.

133

in Normandy, wear large caps or hats which rise quite high and are decorated with flowing ribbons. Large bows of silk, made to stand up, cover the heads of the women in Alsace. The Burgundian women wear small white caps fitted closely to the head and held in place with ribbons. The women of Dauphiné-Auvergne and Béarn wear small bonnets. The men of Normandy and Brittany wear large-brimmed hats; especially familiar are the Breton hat with its ribbon hanging off the brim and the tall straw "top hat" characteristic of the men of Burgundy.[1] Other distinguishing features of the folk costumes characteristic of those worn in particular provinces include the Breton man's jacket decorated with rows of buttons, his pleated trousers gathered in at the knee, and embroidered hose; the looped skirts and drawn shawls of the women of Auvergne; the high-waisted frock of the lass from Normandy;[2] and the elaborately embroidered waistcoat of the men of Burgundy.

FOLK FESTIVALS

As a predominantly Roman Catholic country, France celebrates many festivals which occur on the church calendar. Among the most universally observed Holy Days — hence, holidays, — are: *Christmas (Noël)* commemorated with church services, the traditional and beautiful *crèche* in each home, the singing of old carols, feasting, and the visitation of *le petit Jésus* who fills the children's shoes with toys and goodies; *New Year's Day (Le Jour de l'An)* observed with family reunions, feasting, and an exchange of gifts; the *Epiphany (Fête des Rois)* observed with special parties featuring a large cake of which one piece is saved for the first poor person to come to the door, and in which is baked a small doll with the traditional notion that whoever finds it in his piece of cake reigns as king, or queen, of the festivities of the evening; *Shrove Tuesday (Mardi Gras)* commemorated with a lavish, spectacular, carnival celebration on the last day before the beginning of the Lenten season — a direct antecedent for a similar celebration of the Mardi Gras brought to New Orleans, Louisiana, by those of French descent; *Easter (Pâques)* observed by church services for all. The *Feast of Corpus Christi (Fête-Dieu)* is commemorated with a feast on the Thursday following Trinity Sunday in honor of the Blessed Sacrament by elaborate church services and religious processions, and by the decoration of houses and shrines with flowers.[3] In addition to the foregoing festivals of a religious nature celebrated more or less generally throughout France, each particular village commemorates the specific feast day of its own patron saint.

Particularly noteworthy among the secular festivals celebrated in France each year is that in conjunction with *Independence Day (Fête Nationale)* observed on July 14 in commemoration of the Fall of the Bastille, a significant event initiating the French Revolution in 1789 when the downtrodden and outraged bourgeois of that country freed their fellow citizens imprisoned in its dungeons as a part of their rebellion against the exploitation and abuses of the French court. The celebration of this national holiday includes patriotic parades, speeches, fireworks,

---

[1]Mann, *op. cit.*, pp. 10-21.
[2]"Peasant Costumes of France," *The Folk Dancer*, January, 1945, p. 12.
[3]Spicer, *op. cit.*, pp. 118-130.

French

and street dancing commemorating the *carmagnole* which the French peasants danced while storming the Bastille.[1] This holiday holds for the French the same significance as the Fourth of July bears for the citizens of the United States.

Marriages and first communions, two very important celebrations in the individual lives of the French people, are both observed with social and secular as well as sacred rites. The marriage festival usually involves two ceremonies — first a civil one at the courthouse and then a religious one at the church followed by celebration and merrymaking for two days and nights. A French farmer may be extremely frugal all his life but the occasion of the marriage of a child is a lavish one for which no expense is spared. A dowry customarily accompanies French girls given in marriage.[2] The month of May is known in France as *Mois de Marie* (*Month of Mary*). The people decorate the altars with beautiful flowers and the traditional colors of the Virgin — blue and white. During this month, the young boys and girls of France make their first communions. Throughout the period, one sees processions of children going into the churches, the girls wearing white dresses and veils with wreaths of white flowers about their heads. The day on which this event occurs in each family is celebrated as a special feast day for them and for their friends.[3]

---

[1]Spicer, *op. cit.*, p. 126.
[2]Phillip Carr, *The French at Home* (New York: The Dial Press), p. 100.
[3]*Ibid.*, p. 105.

GAVOTTE DE PONT-AVEN

Gavotte de Pont-Aven is a particular version of the gavotte from Pont-Aven, a well-known town in Brittany. The city takes its name from a famous bridge in that vicinity. In ancient pagan folklore, bridges were important structures which served as localities on which significant events took place. The span of the bridge was considered symbolic of the span of time between life in this world and in the hereafter. This symbolism adds significance to the titles of folk dances of all countries which include the term "bridge" or to the formations such as arches made by two dancers who raise their joined hands high under which other dancers may pass, representing the symbolism of a bridge with its religious implications.

The gavotte as a dance form takes its name from the Gavots of Gap, a city located in the Alps in the upper section of the old province of Dauphiné. It grew out of the *branles* and originally was performed in a circle with a gay, lively style, accented with short leaps or springing steps. In the more recently evolved gavottes, the movement is characterized by greater restraint without a loss of their original lilting quality. Frequently the first step of a gavotte begins with an anacrusis or "upbeat" in the music, thus giving it a quaint and charming rhythmic movement.

While there may be no direct connection between the two, it is interesting to observe a similarity between the step pattern of the representative folk gavottes included in this collection and the step pattern recorded by Curt Sachs[1] to have been used in certain processions in Catholic religious ceremonies in which progress was made forward with a few steps— from three to five—and then backward for a shorter phrase, thus giving the movement a somewhat undulating quality. Other authorities attribute this advance and slight retreat pattern to an association of the step pattern with the movement of the waves against the expansive coasts of France.

Another possible association of the folk gavotte step and the processional pattern mentioned above lies in an almost identical formation of the line or chain for the procession—a staggered line in which each dancer joins his left hand or arm with the right hand or arm of the person ahead, placing him slightly in back and to the right side of the person in front of him.

The simple, but unusual, step patterns of the various gavottes included in this collection —together with the simple design and the haunting, plaintive musical accompaniment with its strange melodic progressions—give these dances a particular appeal in a distinctive style characterized by a delicacy in performance rather than the vigorous and robust qualities which characterize many of the folk dances of other countries.

Formation: Any number of dancers forming a chain by linking little fingers [See Plate 10]. The L shoulder of each dancer is slightly in back of the R shoulder of the preceding dancer. The leader (usually a Man) places his L arm across his back, fist closed, and the last dancer, if a Man, holds his R arm in the same fashion. If the last dancer is a Woman, she holds her skirt with her R hand.

---

[1]Sachs, *op. cit.*, p. 170.

Plate 10

Gavotte de Pont-Aven

	COUNTS	MEASURES
Beginning L, all dance forward following the leader who describes a winding or serpentine floor pattern with		
3 steps forward (L, R, L)	1,2,1	
Swing R leg (knee straight and toe pointed downward) in a small semi-circle across in front of L	2	1-2
Swing R leg back in small semi-circle to R across in front of L to step R slightly in back of L	1	
Draw L heel to R instep, transferring weight to L	2	
Step forward R	1	
Hop R, swinging L leg forward with slight bend upward of L knee	2	3-4
Repeat 3 times		5-8, 9-12
		9-12
		repeated

The dance may be repeated as many times as desired.

GAVOTTE DE PONT-AVEN
France

GAVOTTE DE GUEMENE

Gavotte de Guéméné derives its name from a section of France which appeared on old maps of that country. This particular gavotte has the same chain formation and the same serpentine floor pattern as the other gavottes included in this collection of folk dances. It should be danced with the same delicacy of style.

Formation: Any number of sets of two couples forming a chain in the following order: Man of Couple 1, Woman of Couple 1, Woman of Couple 2, Man of Couple 2. The Men place free hands across their backs, fists closed. Chain is formed with hands clasped as in *Gavotte de Quimper*. [See Diagram 17 and chain of four dancers on French Costume Plate.]

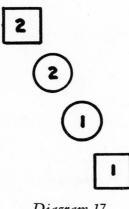

Diagram 17

I

	COUNTS	MEASURES
Beginning L, all dance forward, following the leader in a serpentine pattern, with		
4 gavotte steps as in *Gavotte de Pont-Aven*.		1-4
		1-4
		5-12

II

Women release their joined hands so that the two couples separate, partners joining inside hands. Men dance in place while swinging partners across in front of them. Releasing hands with partners, Men continue to dance in place while Women continue in circle around partners, meet each other, pass by L shoulders to circle opposite Man in same manner and return to original places (as at beginning of Figure I), again passing by L shoulders. Each Woman's pattern is a figure eight. [See Diagram 18]. During this figure, the Men and Women both dance

3 steps (L, R, L) 1,2,1

139

	COUNTS	MEASURES
Hop L, R foot raised slightly forward, toe pointed downward .	2	5-6
Repeat 3 times, alternately beginning R, L, R		7-12

Repeat entire dance as many times as desired.

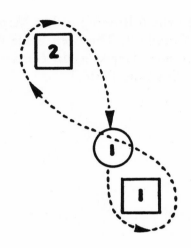
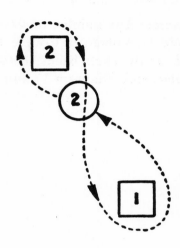

Path of Woman 1   *Path of Woman 2*

Diagram 18

GAVOTTE DE GUEMENE

France

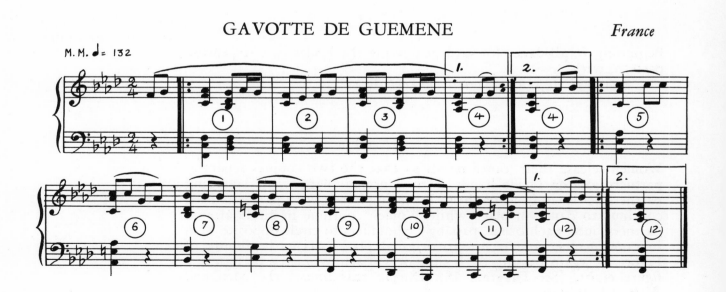

GAVOTTE DE QUIMPER

Gavotte de Quimper is a particular version of the gavotte from a city in Brittany near the coast of France on the Odet River. The step pattern in this gavotte differs slightly from that of the other gavottes included in this collection but the formation, design, and style of performance are the same.

Formation: Any number of dancers forming a chain as each dancer clasps the L hand of each succeeding dancer with his R, palms together, elbows bent with each dancer's L arm resting under the R arm of the preceding dancer, his L shoulder in back of the preceding dancer's R. Usually a Man leads the chain, holding his L arm across his back, fist closed. If a Man ends the chain, he holds his R arm in the same manner. If the last dancer is a Woman, she holds her skirt with her R hand.

	COUNTS	MEASURES
Beginning L, all dance forward following the leader who describes a winding or serpentine floor pattern with		
3 steps forward (L, R, L)	2,1,2	
Swing R slightly forward and back to a position just in back of L foot	ah	
Step R in back of L, bending R knee, R hip directly over R foot, at same time cutting L leg forward, knee straight, toe pointed, knee and toe turned out slightly	1	½-2 (ct.1)
4 steps forward (L, R, L, R)	2,1,2,1	
Hop R, L knee raised in front with the toes pointing downward .	ah	2 (ct.2)-4 (ct.1)
Repeat 3 times	4 (ct.2)–12 (ct.2),	9-12 (ct.1)

Repeat entire dance as many times as desired.

GAVOTTE DE QUIMPER

France

141

BRANLE GASCON

Branle Gascon is identified with Gascony, one of the former provinces of France, located in a triangular area formed by the Pyrenees on the south, the Garonne River on the north and east, and the Bay of Biscay on the west.

The *branle* is an ancient dance form derived from a still older form, the *carole*, which was a dance in a circle or ring. As a dance form, the *branle* was especially popular between the sixteenth and the eighteenth centuries when a series of *branles* were often danced beginning with a stately one and continuing with versions of increasing liveliness until the final dance was a gavotte. Curt Sachs[1] speaks of Hungarian choral dances in the seventeenth century which began with more decorous steps, increased in gaiety and tempo, to finish with something equal to a gavotte in which dancers broke the linked ring to dance as couples, still maintaining the circular formation. The *Branle Gascon* follows this same pattern in that the dance increases in tempo and dynamics throughout the four figures and in that the joined circle is broken for the third figure as partners dance in place with each other in a large circle of couples.

Branle Gascon is, in a sense, a step dance, thus placing it in a broad category of those dances in which a primary aspect is concerned with the sounds which the feet make against the floor. The shuffling, sliding of the feet, which continues throughout the third figure, grows to a rapid staccato tapping resulting from the fast step-hop in Figure IV.

The dance is in four parts, each new part faster and livelier than the preceding one.

Formation: Any number of couples in a double circle facing clockwise, Man on L of partner. The Man presents his R arm to his partner who links her L arm with it. Both have outside arms hanging relaxed at sides.

I

	COUNTS	MEASURES
Beginning L, couples progress clockwise around the circle with 32 walking steps, finishing in a single circle facing in, Man on L of partner	1,2, etc.	1-8
		1-8

II

	COUNTS	MEASURES
In a large single circle, arms extended sideward at shoulder level, hands joined, dancers move into the center of the circle, swinging their joined hands forward and upward and closing the large circle into a smaller one with		
3 steps forward (L, R, L)	1,2,1	
Hop L, raising R leg forward with a bent knee, toe pointed downward	2	1-2
Repeat, beginning R		3-4
Move back to place in the large circle with the same step, swinging joined hands downward and backward and bowing slightly forward on the first three steps backward, the free foot extended backward from a bent knee on the hop		5-8
Repeat all		1-8

[1]Sachs, *op. cit.*, p. 385.

III

<table>
<tr><td></td><td>COUNTS</td><td>MEASURES</td></tr>
</table>

In a single circle, Woman facing in, Man facing out, L hands joined slightly above shoulder level, elbows together, Man with knuckles of R hand to hip, Woman holding skirt with R hand, partners both move forward to make two counterclockwise turns in place, beginning L, with

    16 shuffling walk steps, feet kept close to the floor to produce only one shuffling sound on each step . . . . 1,2, etc.   9-16

IV

L arms hooked at elbow, R arms curved overhead, partners continue around counterclockwise, beginning L, with

    16 step-hops, keeping feet close to floor . . . . 1&,2&,   9-16
    1&,2&,
    etc.

Repeat entire dance as many times as desired.

M.M. ♩ = 126   **BRANLE GASCON**   *France*

LE STOUPIC

Le Stoupic, a simple French circle dance in two parts, derives its significance and meaning from the English translation of the French text for the song to which it is danced. It represents a song and dance by a young woman whose parents are from Locminé, a village in Southwestern Brittany. They have promised her an early marriage with one of the lads from Locminé who, according to legend, have *sous*, or French coins, stacked in the bottom of their shoes. The thought of such treasure cached within the shoes of the potential husbands is no doubt related to the emphasis upon the foot-tapping movement analyzed in Figure II.

The vigorous foot-tapping and arm-swinging in a closed circle offers a delightful contrast to the quieter stepping of the first figure and is especially good fun for any group of dancers. The charm of the dance is increased by the singing of the words in French while dancing.

French Text	*English Translation*
Mon père et ma mère	My father and my mother
D'Locminé ils sont,	Are from Locminé
Mon père et ma mère	My father and my mother
D'Locminé ils sont,	Are from Locminé
Ils ont fait promesse	They made a promise
Qu'ils me marieront.	To marry me off
Ils ont fait promesse	They made me a promise
Qu'ils me marieront.	To marry me off.
Refrain	*Refrain*
Sont, Sont, Sait	Sont, Sont, Sait
Les gars de Locminé	The lads of Locminé
Qui ont de la maillette	Who have the money
Sous dessus dessous,	Sous upon sous
Sont, Sont, Sait	Sont, Sont, Sait
Les gars de Locminé	The lads of Locminé
Qui ont de la maillette	Who have the money
Sous leurs souliers.	In the bottom of their shoes.

Formation: Any number of dancers (Men, Women or both) in a single circle, facing center. With his R hand, each dancer clasps the L hand of the dancer on his R, palms facing, elbows bent. Dancers stand close together, side by side, the L arms resting under the R arm of each dancer to the L.

	I	COUNTS	MEASURES
Facing center of circle, all dance with			
Step L to side	. . . .	2	
Step R across in front of L	. . . .	&	
Step L to side	. . . .	1	
Swing R leg across in front of L, at same time bending L knee	.	&	½-1
Repeat 7 times, alternately beginning R, L, R, L, etc. Finish, still facing toward center of circle and lowering clasped hands	.	1	2-8

II

	COUNTS	MEASURES
All dance in place with		
Tap ball of L foot on floor in front and ball of R foot in place 8 times, balancing on R heel, while swinging joined hands vigorously 8 times alternately *backward* and *forward*	2&,1&, 2&,1&	8 (ct.2)- 10 (ct.1)
Change feet with a spring to L foot and repeat, balancing on L heel while tapping ball of R foot forward and ball of L foot in place, continuing to swing joined hands		10 (ct.2)- 12 (ct.1)
Repeat all, L foot forward then R. On Ct. 1 of Meas. 12, swing hands back, bending body forward from waist in a low bow and hold position on Ct. & of Meas. 12		12 (ct.2), 9-12 repeated

Repeat entire dance as many times as desired.

LE STOUPIC

M.M. ♪ = 112.

France

LA BOUDIGUESTE

La Boudigueste is one of the favorite dances in that part of France known as Perigourdine which no longer appears on modern maps of this country. Traditionally, it is said to have been danced by farm girls at country fairs for the benefit of their potential husbands who looked on as they danced. Since the most vigorous dancers were thought likely to make the best wives, the girls vied with each other in their vigor and coquetry. The girls sang as they danced. The words should be sung in French as the dance is performed. The free English translation of the French text makes the dance more meaningful.

French Text	*Free English Translation*
I.	**I.**
Pour bien dancer la beau de gueste	To dance the Boudigueste well
Faut être Carrabie	It is necessary to be strong
Faut avoir la jambe leste	It is necessary to have nimble legs and
Ne pas être marriée.	Not to be married.
II.	**II.**
Tra la lire, la lire, la lire	Tra la lire, la lire, la lire
Tra la lire, la lire, la la.	Tra la lire, la lire, la la.

Formation: Any number of girls or women in a double line facing each other. Skirts are held high in front with thumb and index finger of each hand. [See French girl on French Costume Plate.]

I

	COUNTS	MEASURES
Women move forward toward each other, beginning L, with	2,1,2	
3 walking steps (L, R, L)		½-2(ct.1)
Scuff R heel diagonally forward across in front of L	1	2, (ct.2)-4
Repeat, beginning R and moving backward		
Move forward again with	2,1,2	4 (ct.2)-5
3 walking steps (L, R, L)		
Swing R leg in wide circle across in front of L, with R knee bent upward and pivot on L, making a half-turn L to face back wall	1	6 (ct.1)
Move toward back wall with	2,1	6 (ct.2)-
2 walking steps (R, L)		7 (ct.1)
Turn L to face front and step R to side	2	7 (ct.2)
Curtsey, crossing L in back of R, keeping weight on R	1	8 (ct.1)

II

Women dance vigorously in place, beginning L, with	2	8 (ct.2)
Step L		
Hop L, R knee bent high with R foot lifted in front of L knee	ah	
Repeat 5 times, alternating R and L. [See French girl on French Costume Plate.]		9-11 (ct.1)

	COUNTS	MEASURES
Make a quick complete turn L with step L	2	11 (ct.2)
Swing R across in front of L as in Figure 1 and stamp R, facing front. The turn is taken with head high, R hand flung triumphantly overhead	1	12 (ct.1)

Repeat entire dance as many times as desired.

LA BOUDIGUESTE

France

JABADO

Jabado is danced in two figures with contrasting design and quality of movement between each part. It is interesting to note that Figure II is danced in quadrille or square formation common to the folk dances of many European countries as well as to those of the United States. However, the style of movement for this figure in which the women progress around the square is uniquely French and a delightful departure from the more usual circular and serpentine designs of folk dances from this country.

Formation: Any number of sets of four couples in a single circle, Man on L of partner, all facing clockwise. Ring is formed by linking little fingers. Couples are numbered clockwise around the circle.

I

	COUNTS	MEASURES
Beginning L, all circle around clockwise one time, returning to starting positions, with		
4 gavotte steps as in *Gavotte de Pont-Aven*	1,2,1,2, etc.	1-8 1-8

Finish in a quadrille formation, Couple 1 facing Couple 3, Couple 2 facing Couple 4. Each Woman's L shoulder is slightly in back of her partner's R shoulder; couples release hands, partners keeping fingers of inside hands joined for first 3 counts of Figure II.

II

	COUNTS	MEASURES
Men move sideward toward center of circle, L shoulder leading, L hand across back, fist closed, with		
Step L to side	1	
Step R across in front of L	2	
Step L to side	1	
Hop L, lifting R foot off floor with R knee bent upward, flinging R arm overhead with fist clenched, and accenting with a shout .	2	9-10

while

Women move forward with Men toward center of circle with		
3 steps (L, R, L)	1,2,1	
Swing R leg (knee straight and toe pointed downward) in a small semi-circle to L across in front of L and back to R	&,2&	9-10
Men move back to place with		
3 steps (R, L, R)	1,2,1	
Hop R, L knee bent slightly upward	2	11-12

while

Women move back to place and progress to next Man with		
Step back R	1	
Step back L, leaving R forward without weight, giving R hand to partner for support on turn to follow	2	
Step R diagonally forward across in front of partner	1	

	COUNTS	MEASURES
Leap to L, then to R in a three-quarter-turn outward toward L, landing on L of own partner and on R of new partner, facing center of set	2&	11-12
Men repeat movement into center of circle and back to place 3 times		13-16
		9-16

while

	COUNTS	MEASURES
Women repeat movements analyzed in Meas. 9-12 three times, progressing clockwise around circle to finish on R of original partner. After the first time, however, the first half of the Woman's step (Meas. 9-10) is not taken in toward center of circle but is danced more or less in place with slight progress to L, gauging step so that turn is danced across in front of Man on the L each time		13-16
		9-16

Repeat entire dance as many times as desired.

JABADO

France

M.M. ♩ = 132.

APPENDIX

TABLE OF CONTENTS
for other volumes of
THE FOLK DANCE LIBRARY

Chapter 4

Folk Dance as a Coeducational and Corecreational Activity

Chapter 5

Evaluation of the Teaching of Folk Dance
    The Evaluation of Knowledge Objectives
    The Evaluation of Skill Objectives
    The Evaluation of Attitude and Appreciation Objectives

Chapter 6

The Production of Folk Festivals and Folk Dance Parties
    Procedures in the Production of Folk Festivals and Folk Dance Parties
    Illustrative Folk Festivals
        An American Corn-Husking Bee
        An English May Day Festival
        A Mexican Folk Dance Party
Appendix
    Table of Contents for *The Folk Dance Library*
    Alphabetical List of Dances Included in *The Folk Dance Library*
Bibliography

Folk Dances of Scandinavia

Scandinavian Costume Plate
Preface
Introduction
    Explanation of Terms, Counting, Music, and Diagrams
    Analysis of Basic Steps, Figures, Positions, and Formations
    Pronunciation of Foreign Words
Presentation of Scandinavian Folk Dances
    Map of Scandinavia
    Geographical Background
    Historical and Sociological Background
    Folk Dances
    Folk Costumes
    Folk Festivals
    Analysis of Folk Dances

Denmark:
Danish Schottische
The Crested Hen
Danish Minuet
Little Man in a Fix
Danish Masquerade
Danish Varsovienne

Finland:
Finnish Schottische
Finnish Polka
Radiko
Kerenski
Kynkkaliepakko

Norway:
Rugen
Tantoli
Ril
Norwegian Varsovienne
Feiar
Little Four Dance
Reinlendar

Sweden:
Gustaf's Skoal
Swedish Varsovienne
Swedish Schottische
Oxen Dance
Hambo

Bibliography

Folk Dances of the British Isles

English, Scotch, and Irish Costume Plate
Preface
Introduction
    Explanation of Terms, Counting, Music, and Diagrams
    Analysis of Basic Steps, Figures, Terms, Positions, and Formations
    Pronunciation of Foreign Words

Presentation of English, Scottish, and Irish Folk Dances

    Map of England, Scotland, and Ireland
    Geographical Background
    Historical and Sociological Background
    Folk Dances
    Folk Costumes
    Folk Festivals

Analysis of Folk Dances

England:

    Rufty Tufty
    The Black Nag
    Gathering Peascods
    Row Well, Ye Mariners
    Hunsdon House
    Bean-Setting
    Blue-Eyed Stranger
    Sleights Sword Dance

Scotland:

    Highland Schottische
    Highland Fling

Ireland:

    Irish Long Dance
    Irish Lilt

Bibliography

Folk Dances of the United States and Mexico

Costume Plate of the United States of America
Preface
Introduction
    Explanation of Terms, Counting, Music, and Diagrams
    Analysis of Basic Steps, Figures, Terms, Positions, and Formations
    Pronunciation of Foreign Words
Presentation of Folk Dances from the United States of America
    Map of the United States of America
    Geographical Background
    Historical and Sociological Background
    Folk Dances
    Folk Costumes
    Folk Festivals
    Analysis of Folk Dances

Paw Paw Patch	American Square Dances
Shoo Fly	Introduction
American Schottische	Lady Round the Lady
Oxford Minuet	Take a Little Peek
American Polka	Birdie in a Cage
Rye Waltz	Ladies to the Center and Back to the Bar
American Varsovienne	Grand Square
The Circle	
Hull's Victory	
Life on the Ocean Wave	

Presentation of Mexican Folk Dances
    Map of Mexico
    Geographical Background
    Historical and Sociological Background
    Folk Dances
    Folk Costumes
    Folk Festivals
    Mexican Costume Plate
    Analysis of Folk Dances

La Virgencita	Las Igüiris
Los Matlanchines	Los Viejitos
La Cucaracha	El Jarabe Tapatío

Bibliography

BIBLIOGRAPHY

BOOKS

Geography and History:

Ashby, Douglas. *Things Seen in Switzerland.* London: Seeley, Service and Co., Ltd., 1928.

Brooks, Robert Clarkson. *Civic Training in Switzerland.* Chicago: The University of Chicago Press, 1930.

Carr, Philip. *The French at Home.* New York: Dial Press.

Encyclopedia Americana. New York: Americana Corporation, 1945 Edition.

Encyclopedia Britannica World Atlas. Third Edition. New York: C. S. Hammond and Company, Inc., 1945.

Funk, Charles Earle, Ed. *The New International Yearbook,* 1945. New York and London: Funk and Wagnalls Company, 1946.

Horst, Louis. *Pre-Classic Dance Forms.* New York: The Dance Observer, 1937.

Kinney, Troy and Margaret West. *The Dance — Its Place in Art and Life.* New York: Frederick A. Stokes Company, 1914.

Kirstein, Lincoln. *Dance.* New York: G. P. Putnam's Sons, 1935.

Rappard, William E. *The Government of Switzerland.* New York: D. Van Nostrand Company, Inc., 1936.

Sachs, Curt. *World History of the Dance.* New York: W. W. Norton Company, 1937.

The World Book Encyclopedia. Chicago: W. F. Quarrie and Company, 1937.

Toynbee, Arnold J. *A Study of History.* London: Oxford University Press, 1934.

Urlin, Ethel L. *Dancing Ancient and Modern.* New York: D. Appleton-Century Company, 1914.

Vuillier, Gaston. *A History of Dancing.* New York: D. Appleton-Century Company, 1897.

Folk Costumes:

Evans, Mary. *Costumes Throughout the Ages.* Philadelphia: J. B. Lippincott Company, 1930.

Haire, Frances H. *The Folk Costume Book.* New York: A. S. Barnes and Company, 1935.

Mann, Kathleen A. *Peasant Costume in Europe.* London: Black Ltd., 1931.

Folk Dances:

Baum, Edna L. *Russian Peasant Dances.* Chicago: Clayton F. Summy Company, 1926.

Burchenal, Elizabeth. *Folk Dances of Germany.* New York: G. Schirmer, Inc., 1938.

Geary, Marjorie Crane. *Folk Dances of Czechoslovakia.* New York: A. S. Barnes and Company, 1927.

————. *Slavic Folk Dances.* New York: The Womans Press, 1924.

Rearick, Elizabeth C. *Dances of the Hungarians.* New York: Bureau of Publications, Columbia University, 1939.

Chambers, Robert. *Book of Days.* Vols. I and II. Philadelphia: J. B. Lippincott Company, 1864.

Eichler, Lillian. *The Customs of Mankind.* New York: Garden City Publishing Co., 1937.

Hofer, Mari Ruef. *Seasonal Festivals and Pageants.* New York: Clayton F. Summy Company, 1929.

Patten, Helen Philbrook. *The Year's Festivals.* Boston: L. C. Page and Company, 1903.

Shambaugh, Mary Effie. *Folk Festivals.* New York: A. S. Barnes and Company, 1932.

Spicer, Dorothy. *The Book of Festivals.* New York: The Womans Press, 1932.

Walsh, William S. *Curiosities of Popular Custom.* Philadelphia: J. B. Lippincott Company, 1925.

Folk Music and Songs:

Botsford, Florence Hudson. *Botsford Collection of Folk Songs.* New York: G. Schirmer, Inc., 1922.

———— *Folk Songs of Many Peoples.* New York: The Womans Press, 1921. 2 vols.

Deutsch, Leonard. *A Treasury of the World's Finest Folk Song.* New York: Howell, Soskin, Publishers, 1942.

Van Loon, Hendrik Willem and Castagnetta, Grace. *Folk Songs of Many Lands.* New York: Simon and Schuster, 1938.

PERIODICALS

Switzerland and Germany:

Alford, V. "Music and Dance of the Swiss Folk," *Music Quarterly*, October, 1941, pp. 500-13.

Barnitz, W. "Swiss Hospitality," *Country Life*, March, 1937, pp. 26-29.

Barran, A. "Autumn Visit to Bavaria," *Living Age*, December 23, 1922, pp. 689-93.

"Bavaria — Happy Valley," *Country Life*, March, 1933, p. 69.

"Bavaria," *National Geographic Magazine*, December, 1928, pp. 679-83.

Chable, Jacques Edouard. "One Country, Four Languages," *Rotarian*, November, 1935, p. 29.

Fuller, R. T. "Arts of Life in Rural Germany," *Travel*, April, 1935, pp. 25-29.

"Happy Switzerland," *Current History and Forum*, April, 1941, p. 37.

Maurice, A. B. "About the Continent," *Bookman*, August, 1913, pp. 635-38.

Medill, R. "Picture Towns of Bavaria," *Travel*, April, 1927, pp. 34-38.

Mimmegerode, F. L. "Beauty of the Bavarian Alps," *National Geographic Magazine*, June, 1926, pp. 632-49.

"Nearby Vacationlands," *Review of Reviews*, April, 1936, pp. 8-10.

Paine, Albert Bigelow. "A Yankee in Switzerland," *Harper's Magazine*, March, 1916, pp. 489–501.

Powell, William B. "The Tyrolean Trend," *Arts and Decoration*, May, 1933, p. 38.

Tarek, O. "Days in Switzerland," *Living Age*, March, 1936, pp. 68-70.

Webster, Princella H. "Switzerland, An Alpine Highland," *Home Geographic Monthly*, February, 1932, pp. 31-36.

Widmer, Marie. "A Little Journey in Switzerland," *St. Nicholas*, August, 1925, pp. 1089-92.

————. "Christmas Customs in Switzerland," *St. Nicholas*, December, 1921, pp. 193-97.

————. "Spring — A Pageant of Folk Art, Flowers, Festivals in Switzerland," *School Arts*, December, 1939, pp. 114-18.

————. "Summering in Swiss Chalet-Land," *St. Nicholas*, September, 1924, pp. 1126-31.

Russia and Central Europe:

Abbott, E. H. "Moravians and Their Festivals," *Outlook*, August, 1903, pp. 809-17.

Bailey, H. "From Peter the Great to Lenin," *Fortune Magazine*, October, 1920, pp. 564-72.

Christowe, Stoyan. "A Rain Festival in the Balkans," *Travel*, September, 1933, pp. 11-12.

Durham, M. Edith. "The Serbs as Seen in Their National Songs," *Contemporary Review*, April, 1920, pp. 831-38.

Fischer, M. "Arts in Czechoslovakia," *19th Century*, November, 1938, pp. 560-71.

Gilmore, E. "Liberated Ukraine," *National Geographic Magazine*, March, 1944, pp. 513-36.

"In Quaint Czechoslovakia," *Review of Reviews*, June, 1932, p. 61.

Jachimecki, Z. "Polish Music," *Music Quarterly*, October, 1920, pp. 553-72.

Jacobi, Elizabeth P. "Hungary, a Kingdom Without a King," *National Geographic Magazine*, June, 1932, p. 718.

Kilenyl, E. "Theory of Hungarian Music," *Music Quarterly*, January, 1919, pp. 20-39.

Livesay, F. R. "Old Folk Songs of Ukrainia," *Poetry*, April, 1919, pp. 24-29.

Masaryk, T. G. "Czecho-Slovak Nation," *The Nation*, October 5, 1918, pp. 386–88.

Mather, F. J. "Glimpses of Russia," *Atlantic Monthly*, October, 1931, pp. 471-78.

Mestrovic, I. "Culture of a Peasant Nation," *Literary Digest*, July 24, 1915, pp. 159-60.

Ogg, F. A. "Slovak National Costumes," *Current History Magazine*, October, 1925, p. 131.

Patric, J. "Magyar Mirth and Melancholy," *National Geographic Magazine*, January, 1938, pp. 1-55.

"Russian Song and Play Festival," *Playground*, July, 1930, pp. 230-31.

Piduch, M. J. "Soul of Poland in Music," *Etude*, March, 1921, pp. 157-58.

Shoults, W. E. "Hospitality of the Czechs," *National Geographic Magazine*, June, 1927, pp. 723-42.

Shoqalter, W. J. "Kingdom of Servia," *National Geographic Magazine*, April 15, 1915, pp. 417-32.

Smith, A. R. "Play in Czechoslovakia," *Playground*, May, 1923, p. 90.

Spender, H. F. "Visit to Hungary," *Fortune*, December, 1923, pp. 951-61.

Starr, L. B. "Nuptial Rites in Russia," *Current Literature*, June, 1902, pp. 677-78.

"Two Kinds of Russians," *Literary Digest*, June 14, 1919, pp. 65-66.

Williams, M. O. "Czechoslovakia, Keyland to Central Europe," *National Geographic Magazine*, February, 1921, pp. 111-56.

————. "Struggling Poland," *National Geographic Magazine*, August, 1926, pp. 203-44.

————. "When Czechoslovakia Puts a Falcon Feather in Its Cap; Ninth Pan-Sokol Festival," *National Geographic Magazine*, August, 1918, pp. 114-28.

Winter, N. O. "Ukraine, Past and Present," *National Geographic Magazine*, August, 1918, pp. 114-28.

France:

Farrelly, P. "French Life in Town and Country," *Catholic World*, September, 1902, pp. 759-66.

Greely, A. W. "France of Today," *National Geographic Magazine*, September, 1914, pp. 193-222.

Holliday, C. "Our Friends the French," *National Geographic Magazine*, November, 1918, pp. 345-77.

Moore, Robert W. "A Skyline Drive in the Pyrenees," *National Geographic Magazine*, October, 1937, pp. 434-52.

———. "Costume Pageants in the French Pyrenees," *National Geographic Magazine*, October, 1937, pp. 435-50.

"Peasant Costumes of France," *The Folk Dancer*, January, 1945, p. 12.

Peixotto, E. C. "French Country Fetes," *Cosmopolitan*, November, 1901, pp. 108-14.

Wood, Junius B. "St. Malo, Ancient City of the Corsairs," *National Geographic Magazine*, August, 1929, pp. 131-77.